Cambridge
Practice Tests for
PET
1

Louise Hashemi and
Barbara Thomas

CAMBRIDGE
UNIVERSITY PRESS

PUBLISHED BY THE PRESS SYNDICATE OF THE UNIVERSITY OF CAMBRIDGE
The Pitt Building, Trumpington Street, Cambridge, United Kingdom

CAMBRIDGE UNIVERSITY PRESS
The Edinburgh Building, Cambridge CB2 2RU, UK
40 West 20th Street, New York, NY 10011–4211, USA
477 Williamstown Road, Port Melbourne, VIC 3207, Australia
Ruiz de Alarcón 13, 28014 Madrid, Spain
Dock House, The Waterfront, Cape Town 8001, South Africa

http://www.cambridge.org

First published 1996
Eighth printing 2001

Printed in the United Kingdom at the University Press, Cambridge

ISBN 0 521 49938 0 Student's Book
ISBN 0 521 49939 9 Teacher's Book
ISBN 0 521 49940 2 Class Cassette Set

Contents

Thanks

The authors would like to thank everyone at CUP for their help and support during the production of this book. We are also grateful to the subject officers at UCLES who have patiently answered our queries.

The authors and publishers would like to thank the following teachers and their students for piloting the material for *Cambridge Practice Tests for PET 1*: Caroline Atkinson, English Language Centre, Liverpool; Mary G. Boyd, The British Council, Bologna; Mary de Freitas, Madrid; Janet Golding, Anglo World, Bournemouth; Alec Ling, Bouzille; C. McDade, Dewsbury College, Dewsbury; Katy Thorne, Teikyo University of Japan, Durham.

To *the* student

This book is for students who are preparing to take the Preliminary English Test (PET).

What does the book contain?

There are five Practice Tests which are just like the real PET. In the first test, each part has some notes to tell you more about it and to help you to answer the questions. In the middle of the book are some pictures which are like the ones used in the PET Speaking test. You may use these to practise with your teacher or with an English-speaking friend. There are also two cassettes which contain all the listening tests.

What does each test contain?

Each test, like the PET, is divided into two papers – Paper 1, which includes questions on reading and writing, and Paper 2, which tests listening. There is also a Speaking test.

How will the book help me?

While using the Practice Tests, you will recognise the kinds of questions which you will have to answer in the PET. You can practise answering them so that when you take the PET you will know what to expect. The Practice Tests can also help you to learn and revise the vocabulary and structures which you have not yet learnt.

How will I use the book?

The Practice Tests will probably be used in a class with a teacher, either with the class working together or as homework. If you are studying by yourself, you will need the cassettes and the Teacher's Book which contains the answers for the exercises and the tapescripts of the recordings.

We hope this book helps you when you take the PET and, if you do not take the exam, we hope you enjoy using it anyway!

Test 1

Notes on Reading – Part 1

What do I have to read?

There are five questions. Each question contains a sign.

- They are signs which you see in Britain.
- They are about things which you can understand even if you have never visited Britain.
- They may be from a railway or bus station, a library, a school, a shop or bank, a bus or train, the side of the road, a car park, or even from bottles or packets in the home.

For example:

was in a railway station.
And

was on a door in a college.

- When people write signs they make them as short as possible, so they leave out some words like *a, the, is, are, this*. For example, the sign in question **4** on page 4 really means '*This* machine *is* out of order. Drinks *are* available at the bar.'

1

What do I have to do?

Each sign has four possible explanations of what it means. You have to decide which explanation tells you what the sign says. Only one is correct. You mark your answer on the answer sheet.

How can I get the right answers?

▶ Read the sign carefully and try to understand what it says. Add the missing words if this helps you.

▶ Look at the background behind the sign. This may help you to decide where the sign is.

▶ Look at the explanations and read each one carefully. Compare them with the sign and decide which is the correct one.

▶ If you are not sure which one is correct, look at each one and decide if you think it says the same as the sign or not. You may then arrive at the right answer by deciding which ones are wrong.

For example: Look at the Example sign on the next page. It was on a door in a college.

B and **D** are wrong because there is no examin*er* in the sign.

B, C and **D** are wrong because they are instructions for people who are *taking* the exam, not for other people.

A is the correct answer. *Silence please* means 'Please be quiet' and *examination in progress* means 'while people are taking their exam'.

▶ When you have decided, read the sign and the explanations again to make sure you didn't miss anything. Remember to make a guess if you really don't know.

PAPER 1   Reading and Writing Test   1 hour 30 minutes

READING

PART 1

Questions 1–5

- Look at the sign in each question.
- Someone asks you what it means.
- Mark the letter next to the correct explanation – **A**, **B**, **C** or **D** – **on your answer sheet**.

Example:

0

A Please be quiet while people are taking their examination.

B Do not talk to the examiner.

C Do not speak during the examination.

D The examiner will tell you when you can talk.

Example:

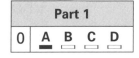

	Part 1		
0	**A**	B C D	

1

A Only use this entrance in an emergency.

B Do not park in front of this entrance.

C Always keep this door open.

D Permission is needed to park here.

3

2

A You need a special ticket to travel on a Friday.

B You can save money by travelling on a Friday.

C Supersaver tickets can be used every day except Fridays.

D Supersaver tickets cannot be bought before the weekend.

3

A Return your books before you leave the library.

B The librarian needs to see your books before you go.

C Make sure you take all your books with you.

D The librarian will show you where to put your books.

4

A This machine is not working at the moment.

B There is a drinks machine in the bar.

C Drinks cannot be ordered at the bar.

D Use this machine when the bar is closed.

5

A This room cannot be used at present.

B This door must always be kept locked.

C Keep the key to this door in the room.

D Lock the room when it is not being used.

Notes on Reading – Part 2

What do I have to read?

You read about five different people, couples or families. You then read eight descriptions. They may be different books, films, holidays, hotels, museums, places to visit, language schools, etc.

What do I have to do?

For each of the numbered people (**6–10**), choose one of the eight descriptions which matches them. The other seven descriptions may be suitable in some ways but only one description matches exactly what each person is looking for. You mark your answers on the answer sheet.

How can I get the right answers?

▶ Read about the people first.

▶ Then start reading the eight descriptions, looking for the things that the first person (number **6**) wants. Mark the information which matches what you are looking for.

▶ When you find a description which you think is right, read it carefully to make sure everything about it is right. If you are not sure, read the other descriptions before you decide. If you are really unsure, then leave that person and do the next one.

▶ Do the same with the second person. You can only use each description once. If you think the same description fits two different people, you have made a mistake. Go back and check again.

▶ When you have found a description to match each of the five people, there will be three left. You do not need these. They are not suitable for anyone.

▶ Now read all the eight descriptions again and check you have the right answers and you haven't missed anything.

What should I be careful about?

● If you do not read carefully enough, you may match the wrong person to the wrong description. If you do this, you have made a mistake, both in this question and the one where the description really belongs. So be ready to check and change your mind if necessary. Leave any people you are unsure about until the end as they will be easier to do when you have decided for some of the other people.

● There may be some false clues. For example, when you are looking for the answer to number **10**, you will find that three descriptions talk about clothes (**B, D** and **F**). At first you may think that they can all be correct, but when you read them carefully, you will find that only one is the right answer.

PART 2

Questions 6–10

- The people below are all looking at the contents pages of magazines.
- On the next two pages are parts of the contents pages of eight magazines.
- Decide which magazine (**letters A–H**) would be the most suitable for each person (**numbers 6–10**).
- For each of these numbers mark the correct letter **on your answer sheet**.

Page

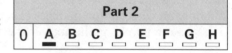

Example:

Part 2							
0	A	B	C	D	E	F	G	H

6  Sarah is a keen walker. She lives in an area which is very flat and when she goes on holiday she likes to walk in the hills. She is looking for new places to go.

E

7  Jane is keen on music. She likes reading about the personal life of famous people to find out what they are really like.

A

8  Peter is going to France next week on business and has a free weekend which he plans to spend in Paris. He would like to find out what there is to do there.

C

9 Paul likes visiting other countries. He is also interested in history and likes reading about famous explorers from the past.

H

10 Mary likes clothes but hasn't got much money so she is looking for ways of dressing smartly without spending too much.

A

MARIA MARIA
She conquered the world of opera with the most extraordinary voice of the century – and died miserable and alone. Michael Tonner looks at Callas, the woman behind the opera singer.

BUSINESS IN PARIS
John Felbrick goes to Paris to see what facilities it offers for business people planning meetings.

B

■ Don't go into the hills unprepared. If you're a hill walker, we have advice for you on what to take and what to do if something goes wrong.

■ We show pictures of Linda Evangelista, the supermodel from Toronto, wearing next season's clothes for the woman with unlimited pocket money.

C

Here and there
Our guide to what is happening in London, and this month we'll also tell you what's on in each of the capital cities of Europe.

Explore Africa
Last year Jane Merton joined a trip across Africa, exploring the most cut-off parts of the continent. Read what she has to say.

D

Festivals
This is the season for street festivals. We've travelled to three of the big ones in South America and bring you pictures and information.

How I got there
Georgina Fay tells us how she became a famous clothes designer overnight.

E

● Read about Neil Ashdown's recent walk along one of Britain's oldest paths. It passes through some of the most beautiful hill country.

● Enter our competition and win a week for two in Thailand.

F

In the Freezer
We talk to the two men who have just completed a walk across the Antarctic.

Tighten That Belt
Well-known fashion designer, Virginia McBride, who now lives in Paris, tells us how to make our old clothes look fashionable.

G

Wake up children

Penelope Fine's well-known children's stories are going to be on Sunday morning Children's TV. We talk to this famous author and find out how she feels about seeing her stories on screen.

Flatlands

It may not look like promising walking country – it hardly rises above sea level, but we can show you some amazing walks!

H

My audience with Pavarotti

David Beech talks to the famous singer about his future tour of the Far East.

New light

Julian Smith talks to the granddaughter of one of the men who reached the North Pole for the first time in 1909. She tells us about his interesting life.

Notes on Reading – Part 3

What do I have to read?

You have to read a text of about 400–450 words. It contains lots of information. You need some of the information to answer the questions. You don't need to understand every part of the text.

What do I have to do?

You have to read ten statements about the information in the text and decide whether each one is true or false. You mark **A** for true or **B** for false in the space on the answer sheet.

NOTE: Statements **11–20** follow the same order as the information in the text. This may help you to find the answer to some questions.

How can I get the right answers?

▶ Read statements **11–20**.

▶ Read the text right through. Mark the parts of the text which you think tell you about statements **11–20**. Remember, there may be parts of the text which you don't need to understand completely.

▶ Work through the statements, checking whether each one is true or false by looking at the text again. Mark your answer. If you can't decide about one, leave it and go on to the next one. Come back to it at the end. It may be easier then.

What should I be careful about?

Read the statements *very carefully*. Sometimes a few words can make the difference between whether a statement is true or false. For example, look at:

> **13** Insurance companies will pay *if someone steals your card* and takes things from your room.

On checking the text, we find that '... insurance companies will not pay ... unless you can prove that your room was *broken into by force*.'

PART 3

Questions 11–20

● Look at the statements below about a student hostel.
● Read the text on the next page to decide if each statement is correct or incorrect.
● If it is correct, mark **A on your answer sheet**.
● If it is not correct, mark **B on your answer sheet**.

Example:

	Part 3	
0	**A**	B

11 Every student has a key to the main door. A

12 You can borrow your friend's main door card. B

13 Insurance companies will pay if someone steals your card and takes things from your room. B

14 Spare rooms are least likely to be available in summer. B

15 Your brother can stay free of charge if he uses the other bed in your room. A

16 Guests must report to Stan when they arrive. B

17 The cleaners take away food that they find in bedrooms. A

18 If you cook late at night, you should leave the washing-up until the morning. B

19 Students who play loud music may have to leave the hostel. A

20 You should ask Stan to call a doctor if you are ill. B

HOSTEL RULES

To make life in this student hostel as comfortable and safe as possible for everyone, please remember these rules.

Security You have a special card which operates the electronic lock on your room door and a key for the main door of the hostel. These are your responsibility and should never be lent to anyone, including your fellow students. If you lose them you will be charged £20 for a replacement. Do not leave your room unlocked even for short periods (for example, when making yourself a coffee). Unfortunately, theft from student hostels is very common and insurance companies will not pay for stolen goods unless you can prove that your room was broken into by force.

Visitors There are rarely any rooms available for visitors, except at the end of the summer term. Stan Jenkins, the hostel manager, will be able to tell you and can handle the booking. A small charge is made. Stan also keeps a list of local guesthouses, with some information about what they're like, prices, etc. You are also allowed to use empty beds for up to three nights, with the owner's permission (for example, if the person who shares your room is away for the weekend), but you must inform Stan before your guest arrives, so that he has an exact record of who's in the building if a fire breaks out. Students are not allowed to charge each other for this.

Kitchens There is a kitchen on each floor where light meals, drinks, etc. may be prepared. Each has a large fridge and a food cupboard. All food should be stored, clearly marked with the owner's name, in one of these two places. Bedrooms are too warm for food to be kept in, and the cleaners have instructions to remove any food found in them. After using the kitchen, please be sure you do all your washing-up immediately and leave it tidy. If you use it late in the evening, please also take care that you do so quietly in order to avoid disturbing people in nearby bedrooms.

Music If you like your music loud, please use a Walkman! Remember that your neighbours may not share your tastes. Breaking this rule can result in being asked to leave the hostel. Musicians can use the practice rooms in the basement. Book through Stan.

Health Any serious problems should be taken to the local doctor. The number to ring for an appointment is on the 'Help' list beside the phone on each floor. For first aid, contact Stan or one of the students whose names you will find on that list, who also have some first aid training.

Notes on Reading – Part 4

What do I have to read?

You have to read a text of about 200 words. It tells you about feelings or opinions. It might be a letter, an advertisement, a review or an article.

What do I have to do?

You have to answer five multiple choice questions. That means each question has four possible answers (**A**, **B**, **C** or **D**). You must choose which one is correct. You mark your answer on the answer sheet.

How can I get the right answers?

▶ Read the text right through. Try to understand what sort of text it is. Look at the shape of it, how it begins and ends, and so on.

▶ Look at questions **21** and **22**. These questions are about the general meaning of the text. Try to think of your own answers first, reading the text again if necessary. Then look at **A**, **B**, **C** and **D** and choose the one that seems to fit best. If you are not sure which is correct, look at each answer and decide if it fits. You may then arrive at the right answer by deciding which ones are wrong.

---

21   What is the writer's main aim in the letter?

    A   to show why her business is successful
    B   to explain why her customers are feeling unhappy
    C   to avoid problems for her business
    D   to complain about the chemist downstairs

22   Who was the letter sent to?

    A   the writer's landlord
    B   the writer's bank manager
    C   the owner of the burger bar
    D   the local newspaper

▶ Now do the same for questions **23** and **24**. They are usually about particular parts of the text. You may need to read the text again to answer these questions.

---

23   What does the writer think about the burger bar?

    A   It will make her lose money.
    B   It will not be successful.
    C   The High Street is not the place for it.
    D   Other shopkeepers will complain about it too.

---

24   Why is the writer worried about her customers?

   A   They do not like eating burgers.
   B   They may not be allowed to use the stairs.
   C   The smells will not be pleasant.
   D   The hairdresser's will get too crowded.

▶ Lastly, look at question **25**. This question may be pictures or text. It is usually quite easy, if you have already answered the other questions, but do look at **A**, **B**, **C** and **D** very carefully, as sometimes the differences are very small and easy to miss.

25   Which of these is part of a reply to the letter?

   A

   Thank you for your letter. I am sorry your shop has had to close down because of lack of business.

   B

   Thank you for your letter. I understand your problem. I will ask them to look at the other shop but I can make no promises at the moment.

   C

   Thank you for your letter asking me to rent the ground floor shop to you. I will think about it and let you know.

   D

   Thank you for your letter. I am sorry that I am not able to lend you the money you ask for.

What should I be careful about?

Make sure that your answers to all the questions make sense together. For example, if you choose **C** for question **21**, you know that the writer is trying to 'avoid problems for her business'. Therefore, it is not likely that the answer to **25** is **A**, because that is about a business which has already closed down.

PART 4

Questions 21–25

● Read the text and questions.
● For each question, mark the letter next to the correct answer – **A**, **B**, **C** or **D** –
  on your answer sheet.

Example:

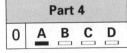

Dear Mr Landers,

I run 'Snips' hairdressing shop above Mr Shah's
chemist's shop at 24 High Street. I started the
business 20 years ago and it is now very
successful. My customers have to walk through the
chemist's to the stairs at the back which lead to
the hairdresser's. This has never been a problem.

Mr Shah plans to retire later this year, and I
have heard from a business acquaintance that you
intend to rent the shop space to a hamburger bar.
I have thought about trying to rent it myself and
make my shop bigger but I cannot persuade anyone
to lend me that much money. I don't know what to
do. My customers come to the hairdresser's to
relax and the noise and smells of a burger bar
will surely drive them away. Also, they won't like
having to walk through a hot, smelly burger bar to
reach the stairs.

I have always paid my rent on time. You have told
me in the past that you wish me to continue with
my business for as long as possible. I believe you
own another empty shop in the High Street. Could
the burger bar not go there, where it would not
affect other people's businesses?

I hope you think carefully about this.

21 What is the writer's main aim in the letter?

  A to show why her business is successful
  B to explain why her customers are feeling unhappy
  C to avoid problems for her business
  D to complain about the chemist downstairs

22 Who was the letter sent to?

  A the writer's landlord
  B the writer's bank manager
  C the owner of the burger bar
  D the local newspaper

23 What does the writer think about the burger bar?

  A It will make her lose money.
  B It will not be successful.
  C The High Street is not the place for it.
  D Other shopkeepers will complain about it too.

24 Why is the writer worried about her customers?

  A They do not like eating burgers.
  B They may not be allowed to use the stairs.
  C The smells will not be pleasant.
  D The hairdresser's will get too crowded.

25 Which of these is part of a reply to the letter?

  A
  > Thank you for your letter. I am sorry your shop has had to close down because of lack of business.

  B
  > Thank you for your letter. I understand your problem. I will ask them to look at the other shop but I can make no promises at the moment.

  C
  > Thank you for your letter asking me to rent the ground floor shop to you. I will think about it and let you know.

  D
  > Thank you for your letter. I am sorry that I am not able to lend you the money you ask for.

Notes on Reading – Part 5

What do I have to read?

You have to read a text of about 100–150 words. Ten of the words are missing. This is called a Cloze test.

What do I have to do?

You have to choose one word to fill each space. Under the text you can see the words you have to choose from. There are four words to choose from for each space (**A, B, C** or **D**).

You mark **A, B, C** or **D** in the space on the answer sheet.

How can I get the right answers?

▶ Read the text right through. Don't think about the spaces, just try to understand the text as a whole.

▶ Look at the example answer (0).

▶ Work through the text, choosing your answer for each space and marking your answer sheet. It's *very important* to look at the words *after* each space as well as the words that come before it.

▶ If you can't fill a space, leave it and go on to the next one. Come back to it at the end. It may be clearer to you then.

What should I be careful about?

Never hand in your answer sheet without filling in an answer for all the spaces. Guesses can be right, but empty spaces will always be wrong!

PART 5

Questions 26–35

- Read the text below and choose the correct word for each space.
- For each question, mark the letter next to the correct word – **A**, **B**, **C** or **D** – on **your answer sheet**.

Example:

Part 5			
0	**A**	**B**	**C**	**D**

SALLY

After two weeks of worry, a farmer **(0)** .... the north of England was very happy yesterday. James Tuke, a farmer who **(26)** .... sheep, lost his dog, Sally, when they were out **(27)** .... together a fortnight ago.

'Sally was running **(28)** .... of me,' he said, 'and disappeared over the top of the hill. I whistled and called **(29)** .... she didn't come. She's young, so I thought perhaps she'd gone back to the farmhouse **(30)** .... her own. But she wasn't there. Over the next few days I **(31)** .... as much time as I could looking for her. I was afraid that I would never see her **(32)** .... Then a neighbour said she'd heard an animal crying while she was out walking near the **(33)** .... of a cliff. I rushed out and found Sally on a shelf of rock halfway down. She was thin and **(34)** .... but she had no **(35)** .... injuries. She was really lucky!'

(0)	**A** in	**B** of	**C** at	**D** to
26	**A** goes	**B** grows	**C** keeps	**D** holds
27	**A** working	**B** worked	**C** work	**D** works
28	**A** behind	**B** beside	**C** ahead	**D** around
29	**A** but	**B** so	**C** and	**D** even
30	**A** by	**B** on	**C** with	**D** of
31	**A** used	**B** spent	**C** gave	**D** passed
32	**A** more	**B** again	**C** further	**D** after
33	**A** edge	**B** side	**C** border	**D** height
34	**A** poor	**B** dull	**C** weak	**D** broken
35	**A** strong	**B** hard	**C** rough	**D** serious

Notes on Writing – Part 1

What do I have to do?

This question tests your grammar. You are given five sentences which are all about the same subject. You have to write each one in a different way but make sure the meaning stays the same. Write your answer on the answer sheet. You are told how to begin your sentence and you do not need to copy these words.

How can I get the right answers?

▶ Read the sentence you are given and think about what it means. Make sure you really understand it before you try and write the second sentence.

▶ Look at the words you are given to start your sentence. These are to help you.

▶ Decide how to complete it. Part of your new sentence will use the same words as the original one and part of it will be new. You can try out your sentence on your question paper if you like. Read it and make sure it really does mean the same as the original one.

▶ Write your sentence on your answer sheet. Do *not* copy out the beginning of the sentence given on the question paper.

What should I be careful about?

As well as correct grammar, your answer must have correct spelling and punctuation. If you copy your answers from your question paper, be extra careful. It's a shame to lose marks through carelessness, so check all your answers very carefully.

WRITING

PART 1

Questions 1–5

- Here are some sentences about volleyball.
- For each question, finish the second sentence so that it means the same as the first.
- The second sentence is started for you. **Write only the missing words on your answer sheet**.
- You may use this page for any rough work.

Example: My sister enjoys playing volleyball.

My sister is *keen on playing volleyball.*

1   Her team won the match last week.

Last week's match *was won by her team*

2   'You've done very well,' said the captain to the team.

The captain told the team they *had done very well*

3   There are three teams at her school.

Her school *have three teams* / *has*

4   She was chosen for the team two years ago.

She has been in the team *for two years*

5   The girls' team has won more matches than the boys'.

The boys' team *has won less matches then the girls*

Notes on Writing – Part 2

What do I have to do?

You have to fill in a form which is like a real form. Some of the questions are always the same. You are always asked to give your name, address and signature. You usually need to write one, two or three words in each space. Write your answers on the answer sheet.

How can I get the right answers?

Learn *your* answers to these questions. Most of them usually appear on every test. Look at the example on the next page to see what you should do.

Name	If the form just says *name*, write your family name/surname and your first names. The form may ask you for your family name/surname and your initials instead of your first name.
Address	Write your address. Make sure it is clear and that you have written enough for a post office to be able to deliver it. Don't forget the town (and country if necessary).
Nationality	This is on most forms but not all. Don't forget a capital letter.
Date of birth	You can write this in words (10 January 1978) or figures (10.1.78). The form may tell you which way you should choose.
Age	The form may ask you this instead of date of birth. You can write in words or numbers – 17 or seventeen.
Sex	Male or female.
First language	Write your language here, not forgetting a capital letter.
Signature	This should look like a signature – as you would sign a cheque or your name at the bottom of a letter. It should not be printed with all the letters separate.

The other questions depend on the form. They may ask you about which sports you like to play, which languages you want to learn, which countries you want to visit, etc.

You do *not* need to use whole sentences.

What should I be careful about?

Write exactly what the form asks you. Make sure you write everything it asks you but do not write more than you need. Write clearly and don't forget capital letters where needed.

Example form

Airtickets Superstore
PO Box 302010   Miami Beach   FL 33118-0220   USA

Name (6)   Marie Julie Menton

Address (7)   49, Les Sources, 86205 Beaulieu, France

Nationality (8)   French

Date of birth (9)   2nd March 1977   **Sex** (10)   female

Countries you may be interested in visiting: (*Please give three*)

(11)   China   (12)   Greece

(13)   India

Probable reason for travel:

(14)   business

Signature (15)   *Marie J. Menton*

PART 2

Questions 6–15

- You want to join a travel club which will help you buy cheap airline tickets.
- Fill in the form they send you.
- **Write your answers on your answer sheet.**
- You may use this page for any rough work.

Airtickets Superstore
PO Box 302010   Miami Beach   FL 33118-0220   USA

Name (6) Gisele Barboza da Silva

Address (7) 107 Church Street, Southampton,

Ham, 3AH 7BH

Nationality (8) Brazilian

Date of birth (9) 11th November 79   Sex (10) female

Countries you may be interested in visiting: (*Please give three*)

(11) Italy   (12) Greece

(13) Israel

Probable reason for travel:

(14) turismo

Signature (15) Gisele B. da Silva

Notes on Writing – Part 3

What do I have to do?

You have to write a letter of about 100 words.
The exam question tells you:

- your situation
- who you are writing to
- why you are writing

Sometimes there are notes or a picture or a map to help you.
You write your answer on the answer sheet. The beginning of the letter is always provided. Don't copy this again.

How can I get a good mark?

▶ Read the instructions carefully. It may help to mark the most important parts.

▶ Decide what you are going to write and *make a plan* (you can use the space on the question paper for this):

- how will you start?
- list the things you want to say
- how will you finish?

This will be just a few brief notes, perhaps only about ten words, but it's very important. If you have a clear plan, you can concentrate on your English while you are writing. Writing your whole answer on the question paper and then copying it is *not* a good idea because this takes up a lot of time and makes copying mistakes more likely. A good plan is a better way to use your time.

▶ Check the instructions again before you begin to write to make sure you haven't forgotten anything.

▶ Write your letter, following your plan. Think carefully about the language you use. Make sure your grammar and spelling are accurate.

▶ When you have finished, read your letter through to check it.

What should I be careful about?

Make sure that your answer matches the instructions and try to write as accurately as possible. When the examiners mark your work, they will give half the marks for following the instructions correctly and half the marks for accurate language.

NOTE: You do *not* have to write *exactly* 100 words. You should aim to write between 90 and 110. As part of your exam preparation, check what 100 words in your writing looks like. For example, is it eight lines, ten lines or twelve lines? Now you know – so you won't have to waste time in your exam counting words. And remember, you won't get extra marks for writing 200 words, but you may lose marks if your answer is much too short.

PART 3

Question 16

- You were travelling on holiday with a group of friends when your car broke down in a small town which none of you had been to before.
- You are writing a letter to an English-speaking friend.
- You want to describe what happened.
- You can use some ideas from the picture.
- **Finish the letter on your answer sheet, using about 100 words.**
- You may use this page for any rough work.

Dear Steve ,

You'll be pleased you decided not to come on holiday with us when you hear what happened!

Our car broke down in a small town, and we had know idea where to go or what to do, because none of us had been here before. So by the time we looked around for some help the shops and garages were close, because we had not choose we went into the cafe had some drink and some thing to eat and I was talking to the ower of the place, when she said the only place we could find to sleep would be the "Grand hotel".

The Grand hotel is very spend and we did not have chose or money, so we sleep in the car.

Notes on Listening – Part 1

What do I have to listen to?

You hear seven short pieces. They are mostly conversations between two speakers but some will have just one speaker. You hear all the seven pieces and then you hear them again. Before each piece, there is a question which tells you what to listen for. This question is also printed on the exam paper.

What do I have to do?

For each listening piece, there are four pictures (**A**, **B**, **C** and **D**) with a question printed above them. After listening, you have to decide which picture answers the question. Mark your answers (**A**, **B**, **C** or **D**). You have 12 minutes at the end to mark them on the answer sheet, so don't worry about this while you are listening.

How can I get the right answers?

▶ The question can help you before you start to listen, e.g. 'How did she travel?' tells you to listen to what she says about different methods of transport. Some questions may help you more than others. 'What caused a problem?' does not really tell you what the speaker is going to talk about but warns you to listen for something that caused a problem.

▶ Look at the pictures carefully before you listen and notice the differences between them. Try to think of the English words for the things you see in the picture so you will be prepared when you hear them. For example, in the example question there are pictures of different parts of the body – ankles, knees, hips and shoulders – and only one of them will be the right answer.

▶ The first time you listen, you may understand what is said but miss the answer to the question.

▶ The second time you listen will be easier because you know what they are going to say and can listen for the answer to the question.

▶ If you don't know the answer, make a guess. If there are words you don't understand on the tape, try to guess what they mean by using the words you do understand.

What should I be careful about?

The speakers may talk about things which appear in more than one of the pictures. For example, they may need to decide about a journey. They may talk about the bus, the train and the plane. But only one of these can be the correct answer.

Remember also that the answer may come at the beginning of what they say or at the end. If you are unsure, you have a second chance to listen and check.

PAPER 2   Listening Test   Approx 30 minutes
(+12 minutes transfer time)

PART 1

Questions 1–7

- There are seven questions in this Part.
- For each question there are four pictures and a short recording.
- You will hear each recording twice.
- For each question, look at the pictures and listen to the recording.
- Choose the correct picture and put a tick (✓) in the box below it.

Example: What should the class do?

  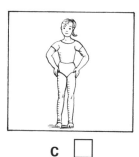 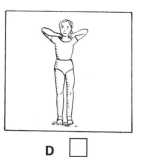

A ✓   **B** ☐   **C** ☐   **D** ☐

1   What is Tim doing at the moment?

A ☐   **B** ☐

C ☐   **D** ☐

2   Which is Peter's family?

A   ☐   B   ☐   C   ☐   D   ☐

3   Where are the tickets?

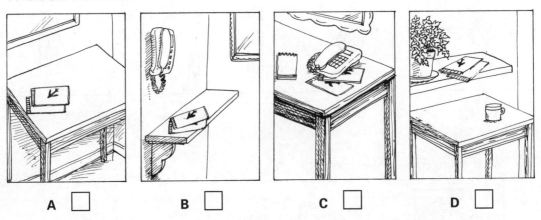

A   ☐   B   ☐   C   ☐   D   ☐

4   What caused a problem?

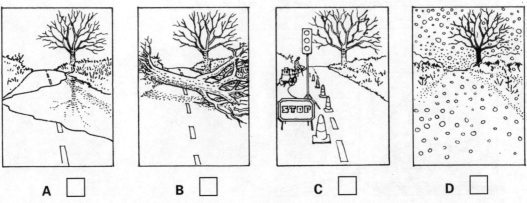

A   ☐   B   ☐   C   ☐   D   ☐

5 What is he going to buy?

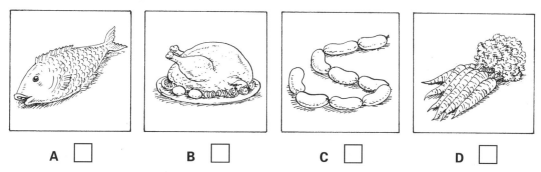

A ☐   **B** ☐   **C** ☐   **D** ☐

6 Where is the house?

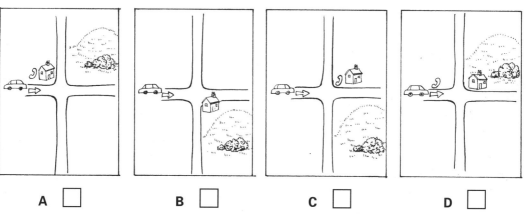

A ☐   **B** ☐   **C** ☐   **D** ☐

7 How did she travel?

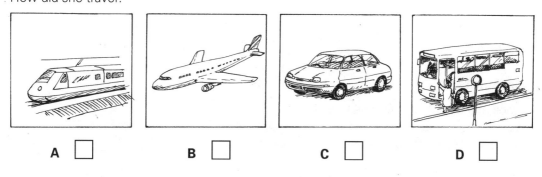

A ☐   **B** ☐   **C** ☐   **D** ☐

Notes on Listening – Part 2

What do I have to listen to?

You have to listen to one person speaking. He or she will be giving some information. You hear the piece twice.

What do I have to do?

You have to answer six multiple choice questions. That means each question has four possible answers (**A, B, C** or **D**). You must choose which one is correct and mark your answer (**A, B, C** or **D**). You have 12 minutes at the end to mark them on the answer sheet, so don't worry about this while you are listening.

How can I get the right answers?

▶ Look at the questions and listen to the speaker. Use the questions to help you understand what you hear. For example, if you read a name in one of the questions, it will help you to recognise it when you hear it.

▶ While you listen for the second time, mark your answers.

▶ Don't leave any blanks.

What should I be careful about?

Don't rush to choose your answer because you hear one word which you think gives you the right answer. Listen to the words before and after it too. For example, if you hear the word *bus*, it may be that the bus is discussed, but not recommended. What is recommended is the *tube*.

Remember also to listen for meaning. For example, if you hear *tube*, the meaning tells you that the answer to choose is *underground*.

PART 2

Questions 8–13

- Look at the questions for this Part.
- You will hear a tourist guide talking about some places to visit in London.
- Put a tick (✓) in the correct box for each question.

8   The guide says you can eat at the Canal Café Theatre

    A ☐ before the show.

    B ☐ during the show.

    C ☐ in the interval.

    D ☐ after the show.

9 What has improved at the Donmar Warehouse?

- **A** ☐ It is more comfortable for the audience.
- **B** ☐ The performers are more famous.
- **C** ☐ The shows are more up-to-date.
- **D** ☐ It is now larger.

10 What does the guide like about the Hackney Empire?

- **A** ☐ its shows
- **B** ☐ its audiences
- **C** ☐ its appearance
- **D** ☐ its television stars

11 The nearest station to the Hackney Empire is called

- **A** ☐ London Seals.
- **B** ☐ London Hills.
- **C** ☐ London Theatres.
- **D** ☐ London Fields.

12 Which part of the Brixton Academy is unusually big?

- **A** ☐ the entrance
- **B** ☐ the screen
- **C** ☐ the stage
- **D** ☐ the sign

13 What is special about Mondays at the Drill Hall?

- **A** ☐ The performers are from abroad.
- **B** ☐ It is only open to students.
- **C** ☐ They experiment with new work.
- **D** ☐ Men can't go in.

Notes on Listening – Part 3

What do I have to listen to?

You hear one person speaking. You hear them twice. Listen to the instructions and read them on your answer paper. They tell you who is going to speak and what they are going to talk about.

What do I have to do?

You have to write the missing words in the spaces. Read carefully as you listen. You will need to write between one and three words in each space. You only have to fill in six gaps so you do not need to understand everything you hear.

While you are listening you write on your question paper and then copy your answers afterwards.

How can I get the right answers?

▶ The first time you listen, try to understand the main meaning of what you hear and listen for the answers to the questions. Don't worry if you don't understand every word. Some of what you hear is not being tested.

▶ After the first listening, read through your answers to be sure they make sense. Read the words that come before and after them.

▶ When you listen the second time, you will understand a bit more. Now you can check the answers you have filled in and try to answer any you missed the first time.

▶ Read your answers through again when you have listened the second time.

What should I be careful about?

If you're not sure how to spell something, make a guess – you may get it right or nearly right and you will still get the mark. Don't panic if you can't get all the answers the first time – you will understand more the second time you hear it.

PART 3

Questions 14–19

- Look at the notes about a competition.
- Some information is missing.
- You will hear a radio announcer giving information about the competition.
- For each question, fill in the missing information in the numbered space.

Competition

Take a photograph showing **(14)** ....

First prize: Holiday at **(15)** .... Bay,
    Jamaica.

Second prize: **(16)** .... worth £500.

Closing date: **(17)** ....

Age: Must be **(18)** ....

Send to DCM Radio, **(19)** .... ,
    Brighton, Sussex.

Notes on Listening – Part 4

What do I have to listen to?

You have to listen to a conversation between two people. They may be
discussing their opinions or telling each other what they feel about something.
You will hear the piece twice.

What do I have to do?

You have to listen to the conversation and read six statements about it. You
must decide whether each statement is true or false. You have 12 minutes at the
end to mark them on the answer sheet, so don't worry about this while you are
listening.

How can I get the right answers?

▶ Look at the statements and listen to the speakers. Use the statements to help
you understand what you hear. For example, if the statements are about
summer jobs and sport, this tells you something about the subject of the
conversation. Try to understand the *feelings* of the speakers. This can help
you to choose the right answers.

▶ While you listen for the second time, mark your answers on the question
paper.

▶ Don't leave any blanks.

What should I be careful about?

Pay careful attention to every detail in the statements. For example, the
statement may suggest that someone *has learnt* a skill, but the conversation may
tell you that he *is planning to learn* it. It's the right idea, but the wrong time. So
the statement is incorrect.

PART 4

Questions 20–25

- Look at the six statements for this Part.
- You will hear a conversation between a girl, Fiona, and a boy, Robert.
- Decide if you think each statement is correct or incorrect.
- If you think it is correct, put a tick (✔) in the box under **A** for **YES**. If you think it is not correct, put a tick (✔) in the box under **B** for **NO**.

		A YES	B NO
20	Robert applied for the job because he wanted to work outdoors.	☐	☐
21	Fiona is looking for a job for the summer.	☐	☐
22	Robert has learnt the rules of American football.	☐	☐
23	Robert can swim but he's not very good at it yet.	☐	☐
24	Fiona thinks that Robert isn't suitable for the job.	☐	☐
25	Fiona thinks she would like to work in the summer camp.	☐	☐

About the Speaking test

The Speaking test lasts about 10 or 12 minutes. You usually do the Speaking test at the same time as another candidate. There are two examiners but probably only one of them will talk to you. The examiner sometimes asks you a question and sometimes asks you to talk to the other candidate.

Part 1

The examiner says hello and asks each of you to say your name, candidate number and nationality. The examiner then asks you to talk to the other candidate and find out more information about him or her. You must also answer the questions the other candidate asks you.

Part 2

The examiner gives you and the other candidate some pictures, drawings or advertisements to look at. Together you talk about what you can see.

Part 3

The examiner gives each of you a colour photograph to look at. You take turns to talk about your own photograph.

Part 4

The examiner asks you and the other candidate to say more about the subject of the photograph in Part 3. You may be asked for your opinion or to talk about something that has happened to you.

Note: If you do the Speaking test alone, it is similar but you talk to the examiner instead of another candidate.

Test 2

PAPER 1   Reading and Writing Test   1 hour 30 minutes

READING

PART 1

Questions 1–5

- Look at the sign in each question.
- Someone asks you what it means.
- Mark the letter next to the correct explanation – **A**, **B**, **C** or **D** – **on your answer sheet**.

Example:

0

A Please be quiet while people are taking their examination.

B Do not talk to the examiner.

C Do not speak during the examination.

D The examiner will tell you when you can talk.

Example:

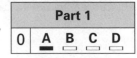

Part 1
0   A B C D

1

A Do not forget to put your luggage outside your room.

B Keep the corridor clear of luggage.

C Bags left in the corridor will be removed.

D Bags will be collected from the corridor.

2

A Do not touch the fruit before paying for it.

B Choose your fruit and then pay for it.

C Damaged fruit must be paid for.

D Self-service fruit is cheaper.

3

A If you spend more than £10, you must pay by credit card.

B We make a charge if you pay by credit card.

C If you spend less than £10, you cannot pay by credit card.

D We prefer cash payment for large sales.

4

PLEASE USE
THE UPSTAIRS
WAITING ROOM
IF YOU HAVE AN
APPOINTMENT
WITH THE NURSE

A Wait upstairs to see the nurse.

B Go upstairs to make an appointment with the nurse.

C The nurse will tell you when it is your turn.

D The nurse can only see patients with appointments.

5

A The library is now a travel agency.

B The travel agency is no longer open.

C The travel agency has moved its entrance.

D The entrance to the bank is through the library.

PART 2

Questions 6–10

- The people below all want to buy a book.
- On the next page there are descriptions of eight books.
- Decide which book (**letters A–H**) would be the most suitable for each person (**numbers 6–10**).
- For each of these numbers mark the correct letter **on your answer sheet**.

Example:

Part 2							
0	A	B	C	D	E	F	G	H

6   Rachel is a photographer. She has a long train journey tomorrow and she'd like a good detective story, if possible one with a female detective, which will hold her attention for several hours.

7   Dean is from California. He's visiting Europe this summer with a guided tour. He wants an amusing book that will inform him about a European country and its way of life.

8   Norman is away from work after an operation. He doesn't usually read much, but he'd like something to pass the time. He is fond of animals and likes finding out about unusual people.

9   Gina is a nurse. She likes to read short stories in her meal breaks. She's not keen on action or crime stories, but prefers something gentler, especially descriptions of people's feelings and relationships.

10   Melanie travels around Italy on business quite often. She wants a book that offers well-organised information as she sometimes has time for a little sightseeing between meetings.

A William Holt
Trigger in Europe

This is the story of the author and his horse as they travelled twenty thousand miles through Europe. They slept over four hundred nights in the open through the four seasons of the year. Over the Alps, the Apennines and the Dolomites they went, eating, sleeping and facing hard times together.

B Barbara Paul
A Cadenza for Caruso

It is 1910. The New York Metropolitan Opera House is preparing a new Italian opera by Giacomo Puccini. It will star Enrico Caruso, the famous singer and friend of Puccini. But murder disturbs the excited preparations, and Caruso's friend is suspected! Can he save his friend in time? An exciting read for lovers of music and crime!

C Alta Macadam
Blue Guide to Italy

This has been described as 'the best guide in English' to Italy. It includes detailed information on history, churches, museums and art galleries as well as some practical information about hotels, restaurants, transport and so on. There are suggested tour routes, backed up with maps, town plans and illustrations.

D Sara Paretsky
Deadlock

Another book starring detective Vic Warshawski. Vic has a personal interest in her latest case. Boom Boom the ice-hockey champion was Vic's cousin. Now he's dead. Vic thinks he was murdered. Why else should her questions about his death lead to other deaths in the Chicago area?
You'll stay up all night to find out.

E Elizabeth Taylor
The Blush

Her sharp eye watches men and women as they go about their everyday lives and explores the mysteries of the human heart. In these short stories, first published in 1958, we see how well Elizabeth Taylor describes hidden depths of feeling and personality with a few perfectly chosen words.

F Raymond Chandler
Pearls are a Nuisance

Three fast-moving stories written by Chandler in the 1940s, including one from the early life of that most famous American detective, Philip Marlow. The reader is carried at speed through his world of dark streets, double-dealing and death by the writer who has been the model for so many others.

G Edith Templeton
The Surprise of Cremona

This unusual travel book, written over forty years ago, is filled with descriptions of people and places in Italy. It is both extremely well-written and full of fascinating pieces of information. A good choice for those planning to visit the country for the first time. It is also extremely funny.

H Margaret Atwood
The Edible Woman

Margaret is an ordinary girl. She has finished university and started her first job. But really she is just waiting to get married. All goes well at first, but there is something inside her which does not want the safe life and the dull husband she has found. A novel which manages to be funny and thoughtful at the same time.

PART 3

Questions 11–20

- Look at the statements below about an Inter-Rail train pass.
- Read the text on the next page to decide if each statement is correct or incorrect.
- If it is correct, mark **A on your answer sheet**.
- If it is not correct, mark **B on your answer sheet**.

Example:

11   There is no upper age limit on an Inter-Rail 26+ Pass.

12   It is possible to buy a pass which will last for less than a fortnight.

13   It is possible to use Inter-Rail 26+ in all European countries.

14   British Rail can advise you on accommodation.

15   The International Rail Centre charges you to plan your route.

16   You can reserve seats before you go if you wish.

17   The International Rail Centre can only plan a route for you if you go there.

18   You can buy an Inter-Rail 26+ Pass at any British Rail station.

19   It is impossible to buy an Inter-Rail 26+ Pass if you have just arrived in Europe.

20   A rail pass for the under 26s is cheaper than for the over 26s.

INTER-RAIL EUROPE FROM BRITISH RAIL INTERNATIONAL

The new Inter-Rail 26+ Pass offered by British Rail International is for people who would like to mix some of the popular attractions of Europe with some of the more unusual experiences that can happen when you get off the tourist route.

Whatever your tastes, and wherever you want to go, people of every age from 26 to 106 (and over!) will enjoy the freedom to travel as they please at astonishingly good value prices – a fifteen-day pass costs £209 and a one-month pass costs just £269. Both give you unlimited second-class rail travel in the nineteen European countries listed at the end of this leaflet. Those countries which are not listed do not recognise Inter-Rail 26+.

Planning your trip

You can get brochures, maps and accommodation guides from the National Tourist Offices for each country you plan to visit. Some of the addresses are listed in this leaflet but we leave all that to you! However, the International Rail Centre at Victoria Station, London SW1V 1JY, offers a special journey-planning service. A route can be prepared, complete with any train reservations that you need, for a minimum fee of around £15, depending on the amount of work involved. Write to the above address, giving as much detail as possible about your dates of travel and preferred departure times.

What else do you need to know?

Reservations are required for certain trains in Europe and an extra charge is payable on some express trains. It is usually possible, however, to find an alternative local or regional service.

How to book?

Inter-Rail 26+ passes are available from certain British Rail stations and travel agents approved by British Rail International. For further enquiries, please call 0171 834 2345 or write (or call in at) the International Rail Centre, Victoria Station, London SW1V 1JY. To qualify for Inter-Rail 26+ you must have lived in Europe for at least six months and hold a valid passport – please bring it with you when you book.

Under 26?

Inter-Rail is available to under-26s for one month's unlimited travel in 26 countries at a cost of £249 – less than £10 per country. Please ask for a leaflet.

PART 4

Questions 21–25

- Read the text and questions below.
- For each question, mark the letter next to the correct answer – **A**, **B**, **C** or **D** –
  on your answer sheet.

Example:

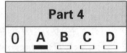

The government published a report yesterday saying that we need to eat more healthily – more fruit and vegetables, less fat and sugar. So that means fewer burgers, chips and fried food as well as cutting down on sweet things. We went into central London yesterday at lunchtime and asked people what they thought about it. 'It's got nothing to do with the government what I eat,' says Paul Keel, a building worker, as he eats a beefburger and chips washed down with strawberry milkshake. 'I think I have a healthy diet. You see, I don't normally eat a beefburger for lunch. Normally I just have the chips.' Any fish? 'I like cod. But I've only ever had it once.' Tim Kennor, a librarian, welcomes the government advice. But he also has his own rules. 'I think,' he explains, eating his fried chicken and chips, 'it's important to eat a variety of food.' We then asked Dorothy Matthews, aged 74. 'I don't think it's the government's business to tell us what to eat.' We went into Simpson's restaurant and asked the manager if people had changed what they were eating. 'I don't think people believe all these reports any more. What they say is good for you in June, they say is bad for you in July. People have stopped taking notice. We serve what we've always served. Almost all of it is fattening.'

21 What is the writer trying to explain in the text?

- **A** what people think
- **B** his own opinion
- **C** the government report
- **D** the popularity of certain foods

22 What can the reader learn from the text?

- **A** what the government is going to do
- **B** which meals are healthiest
- **C** whether the advice will be followed
- **D** what kind of people like beefburgers

23 What is Paul Keel's opinion?

- **A** The government's advice is wrong.
- **B** Fish isn't good for you.
- **C** He doesn't need to change his habits.
- **D** He eats too many beefburgers.

24   What does the manager think of the report?

   A   People don't understand the advice given.
   B   People think they will soon be given different advice.
   C   People don't bother to read these reports.
   D   People are more concerned about losing weight.

25   Which of the following is part of the government report?

   A

   The population of this country should eat less.

   B

   Bad health in this country is caused by people eating the wrong kinds of food.

   C

   People should take the time to prepare their own food at home instead of eating in restaurants.

   D

   Working people should make sure they have a good hot meal in the middle of the day.

PART 5

Questions 26–35

- Read the text below and choose the correct word for each space.
- For each question, mark the letter next to the correct word – **A**, **B**, **C** or **D** – **on your answer sheet**.

RUNNING SHOES

Running is now very popular **(0)** .... as a sport and as a way of keeping fit. Even if you only run a short **(26)** .... once or twice a week, you **(27)** .... to make sure you wear good shoes. **(28)** .... is a lot of choice nowadays in running shoes. First of all, decide how **(29)** .... you want to **(30)** .... on your shoes. Then find a pair which fits you well. Be prepared to **(31)** .... different sizes in different types of shoe. Women's shoes are made narrower **(32)** .... men's and, although most women will find a woman's shoe which suits them, there is no **(33)** .... why a woman can't wear a man's shoe. The same is true for a man – **(34)** .... a woman's shoe fits you better, then wear it. Take your time in the shop. If you **(35)** .... a mistake and buy the wrong shoes, your feet will let you know.

Example:

	Part 5			
0	A	B	C	D

(0)	**A** both	**B** neither	**C** also	**D** yet
26	**A** distance	**B** path	**C** line	**D** length
27	**A** would	**B** should	**C** need	**D** must
28	**A** It	**B** There	**C** This	**D** That
29	**A** far	**B** long	**C** many	**D** much
30	**A** spend	**B** buy	**C** charge	**D** pay
31	**A** look	**B** ask	**C** try	**D** experiment
32	**A** as	**B** like	**C** than	**D** from
33	**A** fact	**B** reason	**C** knowledge	**D** choice
34	**A** since	**B** because	**C** so	**D** if
35	**A** do	**B** make	**C** cause	**D** decide

WRITING

PART 1

Questions 1–5

- Here are some sentences about a film.
- For each question, finish the second sentence so that it means the same as the first.
- The second sentence is started for you. **Write only the missing words on your answer sheet**.
- You may use this page for any rough work.

Example: There is a new film on at our local cinema.

Our local cinema *is showing a new film.*

1 The film is called 'The River of Hope'.

The name ....

2 Our local cinema hasn't shown it before.

This is the first time our cinema ....

3 The main star is very popular.

Everyone ....

4 In the film, he is bitten on the nose by a snake.

In the film, a snake ....

5 The film ends with an exciting car chase.

There is ....

PART 2

Questions 6–15

- You want to find an English-speaking penfriend.
- Look at the application form and answer each question.
- **Write your answers on your answer sheet.**
- You may use this page for any rough work.

English Now MAGAZINE

International Penfriend Service

Full name **(6)** ....

Home address **(7)** ....

....

First language **(8)** ....

Age **(9)** .... Sex **(10)** ....

Please give the names of two English-speaking countries where you would be interested in having a penfriend.

(11) .... **(12)** ....

How long have you been learning English? **(13)** ....

What is your favourite hobby? **(14)** ....

Signature **(15)** ....

PART 3

Question 16

- You have just finished a short language course in Scotland.
- You are writing a letter to an English-speaking friend.
- Tell him or her what you did on the course, how you spent your free time and what the other people were like.
- You can use the information in the timetable to help you.
- **Finish the letter on your answer sheet, using about 100 words.**
- You may use this page for any rough work.

Mon	Tue	Wed	Thur	Fri
Language Lessons	Language Lessons	Language Lessons	FREE TIME	Museum Visit
L U N C H				
Sport	Art	FREE TIME	Language Lessons	Language Lessons
Evenings: Social activities				

Dear .... ,
I've just finished a short language course in Scotland and I want to tell you all about it.

....

....

....

....

....

....

....

....

....

PAPER 2   Listening Test   Approx 30 minutes
(+12 minutes transfer time)

PART 1

Questions 1–7

- There are seven questions in this Part.
- For each question there are four pictures and a short recording.
- You will hear each recording twice.
- For each question, look at the pictures and listen to the recording.
- Choose the correct picture and put a tick (✔) in the box below it.

Example: What should the class do?

A ✔   B ☐   C ☐   D ☐

1   Where is the desk?

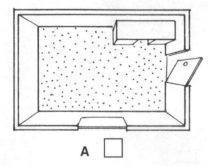

A ☐

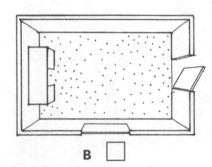

B ☐

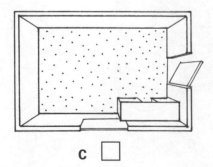

C ☐

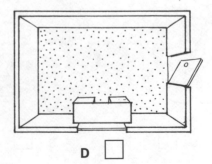

D ☐

51

2 What did he buy?

A ☐   B ☐   C ☐   D ☐

3 How did they travel?

A ☐

B ☐

C ☐

D ☐

4 What does she want to eat?

A ☐   B ☐   C ☐   D ☐

5 What time will they meet?

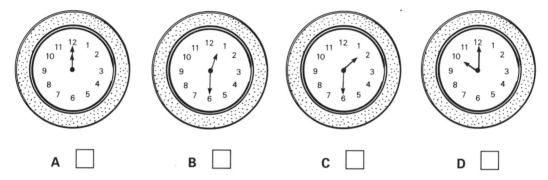

A ☐   B ☐   C ☐   D ☐

6 Why were they late?

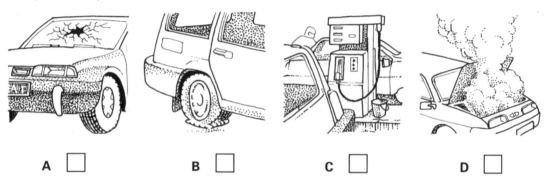

A ☐   B ☐   C ☐   D ☐

7 Where did they go?

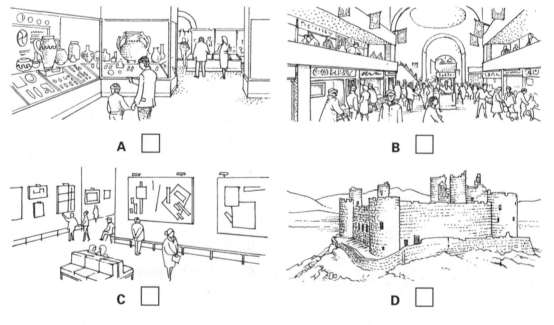

A ☐   B ☐

C ☐   D ☐

PART 2

Questions 8–13

- Look at the questions for this Part.
- You will hear someone talking about a library.
- Put a tick (✓) in the correct box for each question.

8   Monica's working hours are

    A ☐   from 9 a.m. to 8 p.m.

    B ☐   from 9 a.m. to 5 p.m.

    C ☐   from 8.45 a.m. to 4.45 p.m.

    D ☐   from 8.45 a.m. to 5.15 p.m.

9   Staff are not allowed to

    A ☐   bring bags into the library.

    B ☐   bring anything of value into the library.

    C ☐   eat in the library.

    D ☐   drink coffee in the library.

10   If Monica wants to buy lunch, it is best to

    A ☐   go to the common room.

    B ☐   go to the canteen.

    C ☐   go to the town centre.

    D ☐   use the machine.

11   Monica's main job will be to

    A ☐   sit at the desk.

    B ☐   put books back on the shelves.

    C ☐   show people round the library.

    D ☐   send out letters.

12   Newspapers are kept

    A ☐   on the ground floor.

    B ☐   on the first floor.

    C ☐   on the top floor.

    D ☐   in the basement.

13   Monica needs to give the librarian

A ☐ her telephone number.

B ☐ her address.

C ☐ her full name.

D ☐ her tax number.

PART 3

Questions 14–19

- Look at the notes about tourist attractions in the south of England.
- Some information is missing.
- You will hear a tourist information officer talking.
- For each question, fill in the missing information in the numbered space.

Days out in the Arun Valley

Arundel Castle
Open April to October every day except **(14)** ....
from 11 a.m. to 5 p.m.

Boat trips on the River Arun
See town, sail below **(15)** .... of castle.
Departures every **(16)** .... in summer.

Wildfowl & Wetlands Centre
Best time of year to visit: **(17)** ....
Restaurant open: **(18)** ....

Amberley Museum
Open daily during **(19)** ...., from Wednesdays to
Sundays other times.

PART 4

Questions 20–25

- Look at the six statements for this Part.
- You will hear a conversation between a teenager called Thomas and his father.
- Decide if you think each statement is correct or incorrect.
- If you think it is correct, put a tick (✓) in the box under **A** for **YES**. If you think it is not correct, put a tick (✓) in the box under **B** for **NO**.

		A YES	B NO
20	Tom's father is surprised he's in the team.	☐	☐
21	Tom is looking forward to going out with his father tonight.	☐	☐
22	Tom's father is happy to go by car.	☐	☐
23	Tom's father enjoys comedy thrillers.	☐	☐
24	Tom's father guesses about Tom's plans.	☐	☐
25	Tom is meeting the rest of the team tomorrow.	☐	☐

About the Speaking test

The Speaking test lasts about 10 or 12 minutes. You usually do the Speaking test at the same time as another candidate. There are two examiners but probably only one of them will talk to you. The examiner sometimes asks you a question and sometimes asks you to talk to the other candidate.

Part 1

The examiner says hello and asks each of you to say your name, candidate number and nationality. The examiner then asks you to talk to the other candidate and find out more information about him or her. You must also answer the questions the other candidate asks you.

Part 2

The examiner gives you and the other candidate some pictures, drawings or advertisements to look at. Together you talk about what you can see.

Part 3

The examiner gives each of you a colour photograph to look at. You take turns to talk about your own photograph.

Part 4

The examiner asks you and the other candidate to say more about the subject of the photograph in Part 3. You may be asked for your opinion or to talk about something that has happened to you.

Note: If you do the Speaking test alone, it is similar but you talk to the examiner instead of another candidate.

Test 3

PAPER 1   Reading and Writing Test   1 hour 30 minutes

PART 1

Questions 1–5

- Look at the sign in each question.
- Someone asks you what it means.
- Mark the letter next to the correct explanation – **A**, **B**, **C** or **D** – **on your answer sheet**.

Example:

0

A Please be quiet while people are taking their examination.

B Do not talk to the examiner.

C Do not speak during the examination.

D The examiner will tell you when you can talk.

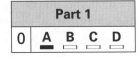

Part 1			
Example: 0	A B C D

1

A We can train you to work here.

B We are not open today because of staff training.

C The shop is run by trained staff.

D The shop will open at 9.30 today.

58

Visual material for the Speaking test

1C

2B

2A

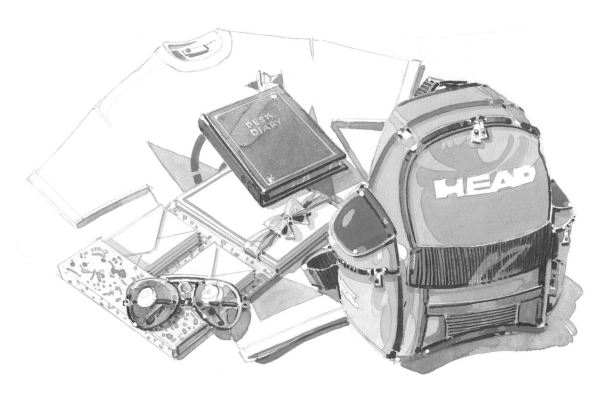

3A

**GORSTON
SWIMMING
POOL**

Opening times

7–10 a.m.
Open for all age groups

10 a.m.–3 p.m.
School groups only

3–5 p.m.
Private lessons only

5–7 p.m.   All ages

7–9 p.m.
Water sports clubs only

9–10 p.m.   All ages

4C

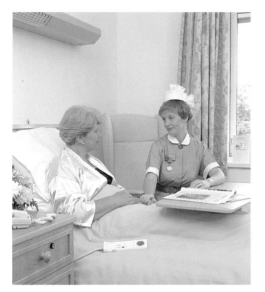

1A

3C

4A

The Pizza Place
Market Square

**Quick snacks
Family parties
Business lunches**

Choose from over 100 different pizzas & delicious salads!

Excellent coffee

From £5 per person

Phone 6060660 to book or just drop in

4B

The Golden Lamp Restaurant
Charnwood Road

LUNCHES AND DINNERS
WEDDINGS AND OTHER PARTIES

HIGH QUALITY DISHES
PREPARED BY A TOP CHEF

WIDE RANGE OF DRINKS

From £15 per person   *Reservations 6061244*

2C

5A

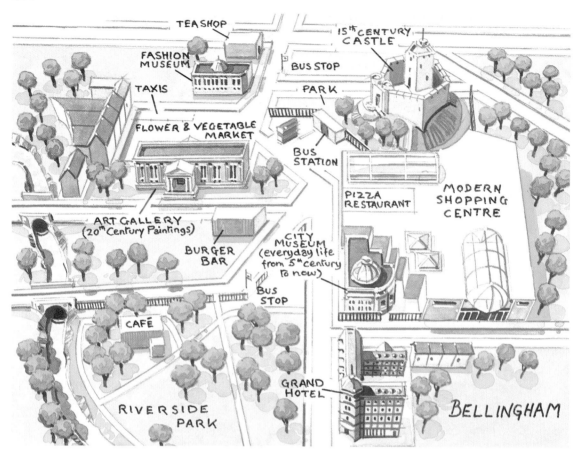

1D

5B

3D

1B

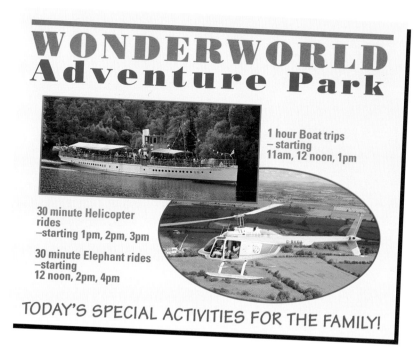

WONDERWORLD
Adventure Park

1 hour Boat trips
– starting
11am, 12 noon, 1pm

30 minute Helicopter
rides
–starting 1pm, 2pm, 3pm

30 minute Elephant rides
–starting
12 noon, 2pm, 4pm

TODAY'S SPECIAL ACTIVITIES FOR THE FAMILY!

3B

May	DIARY	DIARY	May
3 Monday *School 9–12*		**6** Thursday	
Afternoon – shopping		*packing for holiday shopping?*	
Evening – prepare for test		*6pm catch coach to airport*	
4 Tuesday		**7** Friday	
School – end of term test!			
cinema – 4.30			
5 Wednesday		**8** Saturday **9** Sunday	
party preparations			
End of term party 9pm			

4D

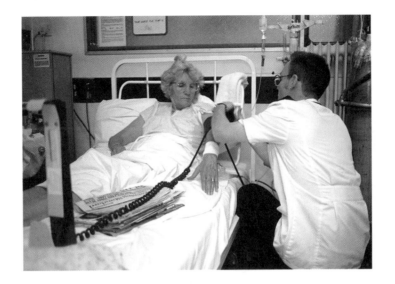

5C

2

PATIENTS CAN PARK HERE IN AN EMERGENCY

A This car park is for patients only.

B Patients can only park here with permission.

C This car park is for ambulances only.

D Patients can only use this car park in emergencies.

3

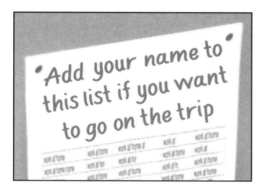

Add your name to this list if you want to go on the trip

A This list should be signed by people wanting to go on the trip.

B Check this list for information if you are going on the trip.

C If you find your name on this list, you can go on the trip.

D This list shows who has been chosen to go on the trip.

4

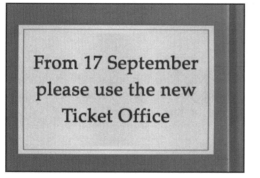

From 17 September please use the new Ticket Office

A This ticket office will close on 16 September.

B This ticket office will be closed for one day.

C The new ticket office is now open.

D There will be two ticket offices after 17 September.

5

WE ONLY REPAIR COMPUTERS WHICH WERE BOUGHT HERE

A Bring your computer here for repairs.

B We will not mend computers bought from other shops.

C We charge to repair computers not bought here.

D Computers bought here never need repairing.

PART 2

Questions 6–10

- The people below are all looking for somewhere to live.
- On the next page there are eight notices offering accommodation.
- Decide which notice (**letters A–H**) offers the most suitable accommodation for each person (**numbers 6–10**).
- For each of these numbers mark the correct letter **on your answer sheet**.

Example:

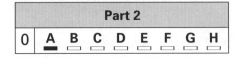

6  Amanda is 19 and wants to share with other girls of her age. She works unusual hours and needs to get to the city easily at all times on public transport.

7  Stephen and Pat live in the city centre with their children. They want to move to the countryside and are happy to drive into the city every day in exchange for peace and quiet.

8  Sarah, a student, wants a room in the city centre so she can walk to museums and art galleries. She doesn't have much money so she is looking for part-time work.

9  Taeko wants to live with an English family and join in family life. She doesn't want to cook for herself. She needs to get to the city centre easily.

10  Martin and three friends are looking for a house or flat to share. They have transport so they don't mind where it is. They can afford up to £1,000 per month.

A Room above restaurant on edge of city available free for person able to work in restaurant at weekends. Area has shops, library, etc. Buses to city centre every half an hour.

E Cottage to rent ten miles from city centre but only a ten-minute walk to local station (journey to city centre takes 15 minutes). One large bedroom. Would suit a couple or two friends.

B House to rent on a farm ten miles from city centre, four bedrooms and garden. Beautiful countryside, lovely walks. Two miles from nearest village with shop and post office. No public transport. £1,100 per month.

C Fourth girl wanted to share house with three others aged 19–25. Two miles from city centre but 10 minutes by train, 24-hour service (we are 5 minutes' walk from station). Near shops. £60 per week including bills.

F Two female students are looking for third girl to share flat in village near city. Own bedroom, share kitchen and bathroom. We have a car so can offer shared lifts to the centre in the morning and evening. £60 per week including bills.

D Would you like to live with a family right in the middle of the city? We are in South Street with shops, theatres, galleries, museums, etc. just a ten-minute walk away. Room available in five-bedroom house for £45 per week – this can be reduced if you help in the house and with children. Cook your own meals in our kitchen.

G House for rent in a small village five miles from city centre. Very peaceful. Hourly bus service during day to city. No children allowed. £950 per month to be paid in advance.

H Room available in family house – £65 per week with breakfast and evening meal included. Own room – share living room, meals, bathroom with family (three children). One mile from city centre. Bus every 15 minutes into city.

PART 3

Questions 11–20

- Look at the statements below about booking a trip to Stratford-upon-Avon.
- Read the text on the next page to decide if each statement is correct or incorrect.
- If it is correct, mark **A on your answer sheet**.
- If it is not correct, mark **B on your answer sheet**.

Example:

Part 3		
0	**A**	B

11   A luxury hotel room for two costs £90.

12   You can go to an evening performance six days a week.

13   You can sit upstairs or downstairs in the theatre.

14   You can eat in the Box Tree Restaurant any time between 5.45 p.m. and 10.30 p.m.

15   Group C rooms are the cheapest.

16   The afternoon performance starts at midday.

17   If there are twelve of you in a group, you can get cheaper tickets.

18   There are two ways of getting to Stratford on public transport.

19   There is one train per day direct from London to Stratford.

20   It may not be possible to go on the day you want.

Stop-over in Stratford-upon-Avon

The easy way to book your theatre seats, dinner and overnight stay

Go to the theatre and enjoy Stratford-upon-Avon's shops, river and restaurants. See Shakespeare's Birthplace, and the beautiful Cotswolds countryside with its charming villages.

For as little as £90 per person in a luxury hotel, we include:

- A theatre seat in the stalls or circle for any Monday to Saturday evening performance.
- A three-course dinner in the Box Tree Restaurant, before (5.45 p.m.) or after (about 10.30 p.m.) the performance.
- One night's accommodation for two people sharing twin/double room. We divide our hotels into four groups – Luxury, A, B or C. Luxury is the most expensive and Group C rooms are without bath.

If you haven't time – or live too close to Stratford to stay the night – why not try our Deals on Meals package which includes a three-course dinner (or lunch if you go to an afternoon performance) in the Box Tree Restaurant. Lunch before the afternoon performance is at 12 noon.

Group discounts apply (15 or more) for Monday to Friday evenings and Thursday and Saturday afternoons until June 18th.

Trains

There is an InterCity train from London Euston to Coventry. Trains leave London at: 9.10, 10.40, 16.55, 21.40. Then take a bus to Stratford. Also, new direct train service from London Paddington to Stratford. Train leaves London 9.18, arrives Stratford 11.30. Returns are available: leaves Stratford 15.55, arrives London 18.15.

Buses

Connect with all the above trains at Coventry Station, journey time to Stratford 35 mins.

Stay longer

You can have an extra night's stay at the hotel of your choice to complete your break. Please note on your booking form if you would like to stay an extra night and include the cost (prices shown are per person sharing a double room) in your total payment. Theatre tickets can also be added for those wanting to go to another performance on the extra night.

Booking is easy

To book, simply:
1. Choose the show and date you wish to come.
2. Choose your hotel.
3. Fill in the form and send it to the Stop-over Office.

Please give a choice of three dates if possible to avoid disappointment and name alternative hotels in the same group when completing your booking form.

PART 4

Questions 21–25

- Read the text and questions below.
- For each question, mark the letter next to the correct answer – **A**, **B**, **C** or **D** –
on your answer sheet.

Example:

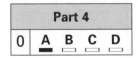

My name's Mandi. Three months ago, I went to a disco where I met a boy called Tom. I guessed he was older than me, but I liked him and thought it didn't matter. We danced a couple of times, then we chatted. He said he was 18, then asked how old I was. I told him I was 16. I thought that if I told him my real age, he wouldn't want to know me, as I'm only 13.

After the disco we arranged to meet the following weekend. The next Saturday we went for a burger and had a real laugh. Afterwards he walked me to my street and kissed me goodnight. Things went really well. We see each other a couple of times a week, but I've had to lie to my parents about where I'm going and who with. I've always got on with them, but I know that if they found out how old Tom was they'd stop me seeing him.

Now I really don't know what to do. I can't go on lying to my parents every time we go out, and Tom keeps asking why he can't come round to my house. I'm really worried and I need some advice.

21 Why has Mandi written this?

- **A** to describe her boyfriend
- **B** to prove how clever she is
- **C** to explain a problem
- **D** to defend her actions

22 Who is she writing to?

- **A** her boyfriend
- **B** her parents
- **C** a teenage magazine
- **D** a schoolfriend

23 Why is Mandi worried?

- **A** Tom has been behaving strangely.
- **B** She's been telling lies.
- **C** She's not allowed to go to discos.
- **D** Her parents are angry with her.

24   Why can't Tom come to Mandi's house?

   A   She doesn't want her parents to meet him.
   B   Her parents don't like him.
   C   He's nervous of meeting her parents.
   D   She doesn't want him to see where she lives.

25   Which of these answers did Mandi receive?

   A | Tell me what you really feel. |

   B | You must start by being honest with everyone. |

   C | Everyone's been unfair to you. |

   D | Don't worry, I'm sure Tom will change his mind. |

PART 5

Questions 26–35

- Read the text below and choose the correct word for each space.
- For each question, mark the letter next to the correct word – **A**, **B**, **C** or **D** – **on your answer sheet**.

Example: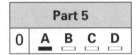

A WELSH FESTIVAL

Wales has a **(0)** .... of about three million. English is the main language and only twenty per cent speak both Welsh and English. Every year **(26)** .... August there is a Welsh-speaking festival. It **(27)** .... place in a different town each year so everyone has the chance for it to be near them. Local people **(28)** .... years making plans for when the festival will be in **(29)** .... town. Each festival is **(30)** .... by about 160,000 people. They travel not only from nearby towns and villages **(31)** .... also from the rest of the British Isles and **(32)** .... from abroad. There are concerts, plays and **(33)** .... to find the best singers, poets, writers, and so on. Shops sell Welsh music, books, pictures and clothes as **(34)** .... as food and drink. The festival provides a chance for Welsh-speaking people to be together for a whole week, with **(35)** .... Welsh language all around them.

---

(0)	**A** population	**B** people	**C** public	**D** country
26	**A** on	**B** by	**C** in	**D** at
27	**A** takes	**B** finds	**C** has	**D** makes
28	**A** pass	**B** put	**C** spend	**D** do
29	**A** our	**B** their	**C** his	**D** its
30	**A** arrived	**B** attended	**C** joined	**D** come
31	**A** but	**B** and	**C** since	**D** however
32	**A** just	**B** hardly	**C** quite	**D** even
33	**A** tests	**B** examinations	**C** competitions	**D** races
34	**A** long	**B** far	**C** good	**D** well
35	**A** one	**B** a	**C** the	**D** some

WRITING

PART 1

Questions 1–5

- Here are some sentences about an airport.
- For each question, finish the second sentence so that it means the same as the first.
- The second sentence is started for you. **Write only the missing words on your answer sheet**.
- You may use this page for any rough work.

> **Example:**   The flight lasted three hours.
>
> **The flight was** *three hours long.*

1   The airport bus is cheaper than a taxi.

Taxis ....

2   They sell duty-free goods in the departure lounge.

Duty-free goods ....

3   There is a post office in the main building.

The main building ....

4   The Hotel Atlanta belongs to one of the airlines.

One of the airlines ....

5   The Happy Traveller café is very unpopular.

Nobody ....

PART 2

Questions 6–15

- You are planning to study English in the UK.
- You want to find a suitable course.
- Look at the questionnaire and answer each question.
- **Write your answers on your answer sheet**.
- You may use this page for any rough work.

---

eea Enford Educational Agency
Enford, Avon, England

Family name **(6)** .... First name(s) ....

Address in home country **(7)** ....

....

Nationality **(8)** ....

Date of birth **(9)** .... Sex **(10)** ....

How long do you wish to spend in the UK? **(11)** ....

What time of year do you want to come? **(12)** ....

Which part of the UK would you like to study in? **(13)** ....

What sort of accommodation would you prefer?

(14) ....

Signature **(15)** ....

PART 3

Question 16

- You are expecting a visit from some English-speaking friends who have not visited your city before.
- You are writing a letter to them.
- Tell them how to get to the college where you study. Say what there is to do near the college, because they might arrive before you are free.
- **Finish the letter on your answer sheet, using about 100 words.**
- You may use this page for any rough work.

Dear .... ,

I'm so pleased you're coming to see me. It'll be best if you meet me when I come out of college.

....

....

....

....

....

....

....

....

....

PAPER 2   Listening Test   Approx 30 minutes
(+12 minutes transfer time)

PART 1

Questions 1–7

- There are seven questions in this Part.
- For each question there are four pictures and a short recording.
- You will hear each recording twice.
- For each question, look at the pictures and listen to the recording.
- Choose the correct picture and put a tick (✓) in the box below it.

Example: What should the class do?

A ✓   B ☐   C ☐   D ☐

1   What are they going to buy?

A ☐   B ☐

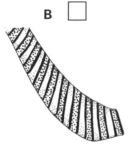

C ☐   D ☐

2 Where is the butter?

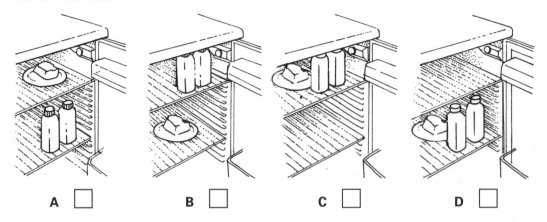

A ☐   **B** ☐   **C** ☐   **D** ☐

3 What does he want to buy?

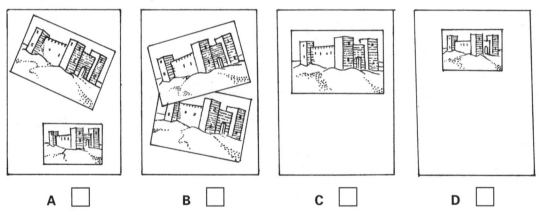

A ☐   **B** ☐   **C** ☐   **D** ☐

4 What is he washing?

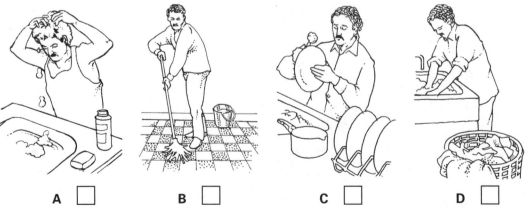

A ☐   **B** ☐   **C** ☐   **D** ☐

5   Where must he go?

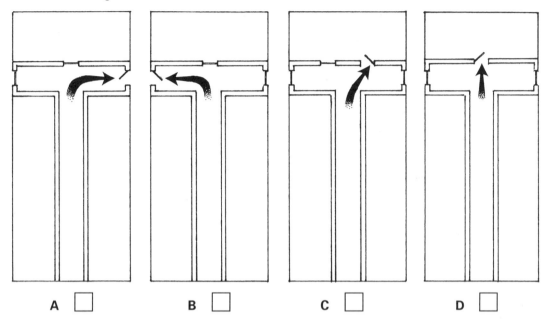

A ☐   B ☐   C ☐   D ☐

6   What's in the photograph?

A ☐   B ☐   C ☐   D ☐

7   What has he hurt?

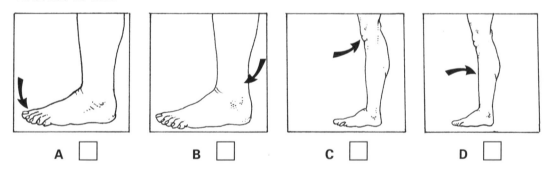

A ☐   B ☐   C ☐   D ☐

PART 2

Questions 8–13

- Look at the questions for this Part.
- You will hear part of a radio travel programme.
- Put a tick (✓) in the correct box for each question.

8 The cycling holiday might be boring for

    A ☐ keen cyclists.

    B ☐ teenagers.

    C ☐ middle-aged people.

    D ☐ lazy people.

9 The group of cyclists had lunch

    A ☐ at small hotels.

    B ☐ in farmhouses.

    C ☐ in the fields.

    D ☐ at restaurants.

10 They felt the cost of the canal holiday

    A ☐ was much too high.

    B ☐ was good value.

    C ☐ seemed cheaper than abroad.

    D ☐ should include food.

11 The people they met on the canal were

    A ☐ unusual.

    B ☐ rough.

    C ☐ friendly.

    D ☐ hard-working.

12 To get a room through the tourist office you must

    A ☐ pay immediately.

    B ☐ book by 4 p.m.

    C ☐ phone the day before.

    D ☐ arrive after dinner.

13 The speaker travels by train when she wants

A ☐ to arrive in the city centre.

B ☐ to visit small towns.

C ☐ to travel from east to west.

D ☐ to travel a long distance.

PART 3

Questions 14–19

- Look at the notes.
- Some information is missing.
- You will hear someone talking about the sports and social club at her place of work.
- For each question, fill in the missing information in the numbered space.

Swimming

Open for our sports and social club:

      mornings – from **(14)** .... to 9 a.m.

      evenings – from 6 to 7 p.m. and after **(15)** ....

Tennis

Book tennis courts with **(16)** ....

Fitness centre

Sign up for **(17)** .... on dining-room notice board.

Clubs etc

Jazz dance society, everyone welcome.

Occasionally give **(18)** ....

Music society – people join to get **(19)** .... tickets.

PART 4

Questions 20–25

- Look at the six statements for this Part.
- You will hear a conversation between Wendy, who runs a clothes shop, and Mike, one of her assistants.
- Decide if you think each statement is correct or incorrect.
- If you think it is correct, put a tick (✓) in the box under **A** for **YES**. If you think it is not correct, put a tick (✓) in the box under **B** for **NO**.

		A YES	B NO
20	Wendy heard Mike talking to a customer.	☐	☐
21	Wendy is annoyed because Mike dropped a shirt on the floor.	☐	☐
22	Mike dislikes having to tidy up the shop.	☐	☐
23	The customer only bought one shirt.	☐	☐
24	Wendy has seen the woman in the shop before.	☐	☐
25	Mike refuses to accept Wendy's advice.	☐	☐

About the Speaking test

The Speaking test lasts about 10 or 12 minutes. You usually do the Speaking test at the same time as another candidate. There are two examiners but probably only one of them will talk to you. The examiner sometimes asks you a question and sometimes asks you to talk to the other candidate.

Part 1

The examiner says hello and asks each of you to say your name, candidate number and nationality. The examiner then asks you to talk to the other candidate and find out more information about him or her. You must also answer the questions the other candidate asks you.

Part 2

The examiner gives you and the other candidate some pictures, drawings or advertisements to look at. Together you talk about what you can see.

Part 3

The examiner gives each of you a colour photograph to look at. You take turns to talk about your own photograph.

Part 4

The examiner asks you and the other candidate to say more about the subject of the photograph in Part 3. You may be asked for your opinion or to talk about something that has happened to you.

Note: If you do the Speaking test alone, it it is similar but you talk to the examiner instead of another candidate.

Test 4

PAPER 1   Reading and Writing Test   1 hour 30 minutes

READING

PART 1

Questions 1–5

- Look at the sign in each question.
- Someone asks you what it means.
- Mark the letter next to the correct explanation – **A**, **B**, **C** or **D** – **on your answer sheet**.

Example:

0

A Please be quiet while people are taking their examination.

B Do not talk to the examiner.

C Do not speak during the examination.

D The examiner will tell you when you can talk.

Example:

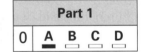

Part 1			
0	**A**	**B** **C** **D**

1

A You can only buy single tickets on this bus.

B You can only buy tickets at the bus station.

C Return tickets must always be shown.

D A return ticket will save you money on this bus.

2

A Latecomers must sit at the back.

B Latecomers must wait on the stairs.

C If you are late, you must use a different entrance.

D If you are late, you must go back to the entrance.

3

A We are now open all weekend.

B On Saturdays we are now open in the afternoon instead of the morning.

C On Saturdays we now close for lunch.

D On Saturdays we now stay open longer than before.

4

A We must see your discount card before we reduce the price of goods.

B We can only give a discount on certain goods.

C We are selling cards at reduced prices.

D We can sell you a discount card here.

5

A Tell the receptionist when you want to see the doctor.

B The receptionist will tell you where to buy medicines.

C If you need more medicine, see the receptionist.

D Give your prescription to the receptionist to check.

PART 2

Questions 6–10

- The people below all want to study English.
- On the next page there are details of eight language courses.
- Decide which course (**letters A–H**) would be the most suitable for each person (**numbers 6–10**).
- For each of these numbers mark the correct letter **on your answer sheet**.

Example:

Part 2							
0	A	B	C	D	E	F	G	H

6 Ibrahim is a journalist. He knows quite a lot of English, but he wants to improve his writing skills. He works long hours on weekdays at an office in London.

7 Siv is going to university in Sweden next year and wants to spend this year improving her English. She wants to meet people from other parts of the world and have a good social life.

8 Maria is 45. She would like to follow an individual course of study somewhere quiet and comfortable with a private teacher.

9 Chang is visiting England for the first time this summer. He'll stay a month and hopes to make new friends, but is rather shy, so he'd like a school with lots of out-of-class activities.

10 Vera lives with a family in London and looks after their little girls during the day. She studies on her own but also needs a language course that will help her prepare for her exams.

A BESTON HALL
Summer special

A six-week programme of classes covering all aspects of English, both spoken and written, for serious students whether beginners, intermediate or advanced. At least six hours' teaching every day except Sundays, plus individual work plans on topics of special interest.

B BESTON HALL
Summer holiday courses

Three-week, one-month or six-week courses for students of all standards, which combine daily language classes with a full programme of sports (tennis, swimming, volleyball, etc.), social activities (discos, quizzes, film club, etc.) and outings (London, Stratford-upon-Avon, Bath, etc.).

C LONDON LANGUAGES
Business Department

Courses in most European languages are offered for adults wishing to study outside office hours, including weekends. Our qualified teachers are always native speakers, whether of Danish, English or Greek. You will study hard in very small groups with lots of attention to individual needs. Courses last between three and six months.

D LONDON LANGUAGES
Part-time courses

Morning classes 15 hours per week, afternoon classes 15 hours per week. Examination preparation 4 or 6 hours per week, afternoons or evenings. All teachers highly experienced and well qualified. Minimum course one month. Central location, easy access by bus or underground.

E LONDON LANGUAGES
Home from home

We place students with experienced and qualified teachers throughout Britain for individual study programmes in the teacher's own home. An excellent choice for those who wish to improve their English fast, but who are not keen on returning to the classroom. High standards of comfort, in a friendly but peaceful atmosphere.

F LONDON LANGUAGES
Pre-sessional course

Organised in conjunction with a number of leading UK universities, this one-month course (1st–30th September) is for overseas students who need to improve their English language skills before beginning a UK university course. Hard work, but with excellent results!

G ELGIN HOUSE SCHOOL

This excellent school in an attractive suburb of Brighton offers courses in general English from three to twelve months. Accommodation is carefully chosen and the school is famous for its programme of activities beyond the classroom. Teenagers and young adults come to us from over thirty different countries to study hard and enjoy themselves too.

H CRAWFORD'S LANGUAGE ACADEMY

This small school offers a wide range of courses, both half-day and evenings, from five to fifteen hours per week. In an attractive building near Edinburgh's main business centre, it is easy to reach by public transport. Modern equipment and experienced staff make it an obvious choice for any business person or student studying English in Scotland.

PART 3

Questions 11–20

- Look at the statements below about entertainment for children in London.
- Read the text on the next page to decide if each statement is correct or incorrect.
- If it is correct, mark **A on your answer sheet**.
- If it is not correct, mark **B on your answer sheet**.

Example:

11 The Barbican Centre programme changes from day to day.

12 Children can be left at the Barbican Centre for the day.

13 At the South Bank Centre there is dance from different parts of the world.

14 The Children's Zoo sells soft toy animals.

15 At the Tower Hill Pageant visitors can learn about the past.

16 Children can learn traditional music with the Town Crier.

17 Visitors to the Museum of the Moving Image can watch actors making a film.

18 The Museum of the Moving Image is most suitable for older children.

19 The Jumping Jelly Bean Club is in a hotel.

20 It costs £3.95 to join the Jumping Jelly Bean Club.

Visiting London with children? Here's a guide to some attractions for younger tourists.

The **Barbican Centre** has its annual children's festival, *Summer in the City*, on 1–5 August. Each day's timetable is handed out as you enter. It may include magic shows, face painting, hat making and music. One ticket (£4.50 for children, £1 for adults, and no children or adults allowed on their own) buys a full day's activity so you can have a go at everything.

At the **South Bank Centre** young dancers can join in *Sleeping Beauty* workshops with the English National Ballet on 3 August. On 4 August Peter Badejo encourages all comers to join in African dance and there's outdoor dance, theatre and music for all the family on the terraces around the Centre at weekends. For example, on 21 August the *Teatro Buendia* from Cuba will present a show for children of all ages called *An Elephant Takes Too Much Room*.

At **London Zoo** there is a special exhibition about animals which have disappeared as well as animals in danger of disappearing. There are life-size moving models of dinosaurs, but you can also see living examples of endangered species such as tigers and bird-eating spiders. While you may not want to get too near these, there are plenty of friendly animals in the new Children's Zoo which will be happy to let you get close to them.

The **Tower Hill Pageant** is a dark ride museum showing the history of the City of London. Outside, the Town Crier calls visitors to *Coin Striking* when children can beat out copies of old coins in metal using traditional methods. Musicians and street performers will also be appearing throughout the summer.

The **Museum of the Moving Image** is about the cinema. Its guides are actors dressed as cowboys and film stars. You can learn about film-making in special classes and there is a special exhibition at eye-level for very young children under one metre tall.

If adults are ready for a rest why not book Sunday lunch at the Russell Hotel? The **Jumping Jelly Bean Club** offers an exercise class (with qualified instructors) for children while you have a drink. Sit down to lunch together (£14.25 for adults, £3.95 for the children's menu), then while you have your coffee, the Jumping Jelly Beaners watch children's films. The Club is held every Sunday lunchtime and it's free to children with families eating in the hotel.

PART 4

Questions 21–25

- Read the text and questions below.
- For each question, mark the letter next to the correct answer – **A, B, C or D** – **on your answer sheet**.

Example:

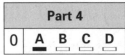

There's an old saying in the theatre world – 'Never work with children or animals'. It's a pity that Herman Gross has never heard this piece of advice, or if he has, that he didn't pay attention to it. It's not so much that *Pet Doctor* is a bad film, although I can't really find many reasons for saying it's a good one. It's more that it makes me angry. Gross is a good actor. His appearance on the New York stage last winter in Shakespeare's *Romeo and Juliet* showed that he really can act. So what's he doing in this nonsense?

It's a story about a small town doctor who finds he's making more money by looking after the local children's pets than he is by looking after humans. Then he gets into trouble with the police, because he doesn't have the right sort of licence to do this and, surprise, surprise, the children and their pets find a way to solve his problems. I won't say how, as it's the only part of the film that's even slightly original or amusing. If you have to see it, you'd be annoyed with me for telling you. But my advice is, when it comes to a cinema near you – stay in and shampoo the cat.

21 What is the writer trying to do in the text?

    A   compare the theatre and the cinema
    B   compare Herman Gross with another actor
    C   give his or her opinion about using animals in films
    D   give his or her opinion about *Pet Doctor*

22 What would a reader expect to get from this text?

    A   information about a new film
    B   ideas about how animals should be cared for
    C   news about the lives of film stars
    D   information about the careers of child actors

23 How did the writer feel about *Pet Doctor*?

    A   It's funny.
    B   It ends too suddenly.
    C   It's not worth seeing.
    D   It's ideal family entertainment.

24   Why did the writer mention *Romeo and Juliet*?

    A   It's an example of a really good play.
    B   Gross proved he's a good actor in it.
    C   It was produced in New York.
    D   The central characters are very young.

25   Which one of these TV guides is describing *Pet Doctor*?

A

7pm A doctor's patients complain about him. He is reported to the police and he has a lot of explaining to do.

B

7pm A doctor prefers animals to humans and stops looking after his patients. People are dying, the animals are cured, then the police arrive ...

C

7pm A doctor finds he can cure local animals, then discovers this isn't allowed. But it all finishes happily.

D

7pm A doctor is loved by the children whose pets he cures. But everything goes wrong and he is sent to prison.

PART 5

Questions 26–35

- Read the text below and choose the correct word for each space.
- For each question, mark the letter next to the correct word – **A**, **B**, **C**, or **D** – **on your answer sheet**.

Example:

Part 5
0   <u>A</u>   B   C   D

FURTHER EDUCATION

Around the age of sixteen you must make one of the biggest decisions **(0)** .... your life. Do I stay on at school and hopefully go on to university **(26)** ....? Do I leave and start work or begin a training **(27)** ....? The decision is yours, but it may be **(28)** .... remembering two things: there's more unemployment **(29)** .... people who haven't been to university, and people who have the right **(30)** .... will have a big advantage in the competition for jobs.

If you decide to go **(31)** .... into a job, there are many opportunities for training. Getting qualifications will **(32)** .... you to get on more quickly in many careers, and evening classes allow you to learn **(33)** .... you earn. Starting work and taking a break to study when you're older is **(34)** .... possibility. This way, you can save up money for your student days, as well as **(35)** .... practical work experience.

---

(0)	**A** of	**B** to	**C** with	**D** for
26	**A** after	**B** later	**C** then	**D** past
27	**A** school	**B** class	**C** course	**D** term
28	**A** worth	**B** necessary	**C** important	**D** useful
29	**A** between	**B** among	**C** with	**D** through
30	**A** notes	**B** papers	**C** arts	**D** skills
31	**A** straight	**B** just	**C** direct	**D** rather
32	**A** make	**B** help	**C** let	**D** give
33	**A** where	**B** while	**C** when	**D** what
34	**A** also	**B** again	**C** another	**D** always
35	**A** getting	**B** making	**C** taking	**D** doing

WRITING

PART 1

Questions 1–5

- Here are some sentences about medicine.
- For each question, finish the second sentence so that it means the same as the first.
- The second sentence is started for you. **Write only the missing words on your answer sheet**.
- You may use this page for any rough work.

Example: The hospital is near the city centre.

The hospital is not *far from the city centre.*

1   The doctor hasn't enough time to see you now.

The doctor is too ....

2   The new hospital is bigger than the old one.

The old hospital was ....

3   The doctor is not available on Sundays.

You can't ....

4   You don't need an appointment on Saturdays.

Appointments aren't ....

5   You should take these tablets after meals.

These tablets ....

PART 2

Questions 6–15

- You would like to join a sports club while you are staying in England.
- Look at the application form and answer each question.
- **Write your answers on your answer sheet**.
- You may use this page for any rough work.

HUNSTABLE CITY SPORTS CLUB
12, Park View, Hunstable

Surname **(6)** .... Initials ....

Date of birth **(7)** .... Sex **(8)** ....

Home address **(9)**

....

....

Nationality **(10)** ....

Where do you practise sports at present?

(11) ....

Sports you are interested in playing: *(Please name two)*

(12) .... **(13)** ....

How many times a week will you want to use the sports centre?

(14) ....

Signature **(15)** ....

PART 3

Question 16

- You have seen an advertisement in the newspaper and are interested in the job.
- You are writing a letter to Mr Stevens.
- Tell him about yourself.
- You should use the advertisement to help you.
- **Finish the letter on your answer sheet, using about 100 words.**
- You may use this page for any rough work.

WINFIELD CONFERENCE CENTRE

BRIGHT person needed
Friday–Monday to help organiser of
international conferences. Some
knowledge of English helpful.
Pleasant, friendly manner essential.

Write, giving full details about yourself
to: Mr M. J. Stevens,
Winfield Conference Centre, PO Box 45

Dear Mr Stevens,

I have seen your advertisement in the newspaper and I would very much like to work with you.

....

....

....

....

....

....

....

....

....

PAPER 2   Listening Test   Approx 30 minutes
(+12 minutes transfer time)

PART 1

Questions 1–7

- There are seven questions in this Part.
- For each question there are four pictures and a short recording.
- You will hear each recording twice.
- For each question, look at the pictures and listen to the recording.
- Choose the correct picture and put a tick (✔) in the box below it.

Example: What should the class do?

A ✔   B ☐   C ☐   D ☐

1   Which mug did he get?

A ☐   B ☐

C ☐   D ☐

2   What has arrived?

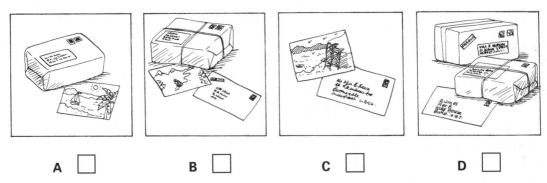

A ☐   B ☐   C ☐   D ☐

3   Which sport is she training for?

A ☐   B ☐   C ☐   D ☐

4   How will she travel?

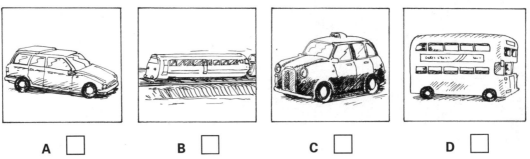

A ☐   B ☐   C ☐   D ☐

5   What does he want to buy?

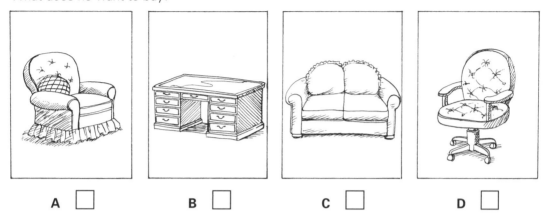

A ☐   **B** ☐   **C** ☐   **D** ☐

6   Which door can she use?

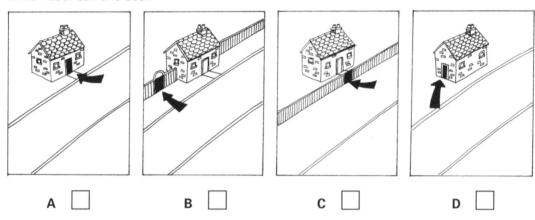

A ☐   **B** ☐   **C** ☐   **D** ☐

7   What has she been doing?

A ☐   **B** ☐   **C** ☐   **D** ☐

PART 2

Questions 8–13

- Look at the questions for this Part.
- You will hear some travel news on the radio.
- Put a tick (✔) in the correct box for each question.

8 What started the problems in Appletree Avenue?

    A ☐ engineering work

    B ☐ a road accident

    C ☐ bad weather

    D ☐ an old bridge

9 Where can traffic only move in one direction?

    A ☐ part of London Road

    B ☐ between the High Street and London Road

    C ☐ the north end of the High Street

    D ☐ both London Road and the High Street

10 The pavement in River Street is covered with

    A ☐ builder's equipment.

    B ☐ a broken wall.

    C ☐ sports equipment.

    D ☐ a new building.

11 Who plans to walk round the city centre tomorrow?

    A ☐ the mayor

    B ☐ some officials

    C ☐ college students

    D ☐ a government minister

12 What will the weather be like tomorrow?

    A ☐ cool

    B ☐ foggy

    C ☐ wet

    D ☐ warm

13 What time is the next travel news?

A ☐ one o'clock

B ☐ eight o'clock

C ☐ ten past eight

D ☐ eighteen minutes past eight

PART 3

Questions 14–19

- Look at Polly's notes about a camping trip with her friend Sue.
- Some information is missing.
- You will hear Sue talking to Polly.
- For each question, fill in the missing information in the numbered space.

Next weekend

Camping with Sue! From Friday p.m. till Monday a.m.

Campsite near **(14)** .... in Wales.

Transport: **(15)** .... and then **(16)** ....

Remember to bring **(17)** .... and **(18)** ....

Meet Sue in bus station at **(19)** .... on Friday.

PART 4

Questions 20–25

- Look at the six statements for this Part.
- You will hear a conversation between a man, David, and a woman, Anne, who have just returned from holiday.
- Decide if you think each statement is correct or incorrect.
- If you think it is correct, put a tick (✔) in the box under **A** for **YES**. If you think it is not correct, put a tick (✔) in the box under **B** for **NO**.

		A YES	B NO
20	They can't drink the milk.	☐	☐
21	Anne was hoping to have a sandwich.	☐	☐
22	They had forgotten the freezer was empty.	☐	☐
23	Richard normally lives somewhere else.	☐	☐
24	Anne thinks Richard will be able to explain everything.	☐	☐
25	David will talk to Richard on the phone.	☐	☐

About the Speaking test

The Speaking test lasts about 10 or 12 minutes. You usually do the Speaking test at the same time as another candidate. There are two examiners but probably only one of them will talk to you. The examiner sometimes asks you a question and sometimes asks you to talk to the other candidate.

Part 1

The examiner says hello and asks each of you to say your name, candidate number and nationality. The examiner then asks you to talk to the other candidate and find out more information about him or her. You must also answer the questions the other candidate asks you.

Part 2

The examiner gives you and the other candidate some pictures, drawings or advertisements to look at. Together you talk about what you can see.

Part 3

The examiner gives each of you a colour photograph to look at. You take turns to talk about your own photograph.

Part 4

The examiner asks you and the other candidate to say more about the subject of the photograph in Part 3. You may be asked for your opinion or to talk about something that has happened to you.

Note: If you do the Speaking test alone, it is similar but you talk to the examiner instead of another candidate.

Test 5

PAPER 1   Reading and Writing Test   1 hour 30 minutes

READING

PART 1

Questions 1–5

- Look at the sign in each question.
- Someone asks you what it means.
- Mark the letter next to the correct explanation – **A**, **B**, **C** or **D** – **on your answer sheet.**

Example:

0

A Please be quiet while people are taking their examination.

B Do not talk to the examiner.

C Do not speak during the examination.

D The examiner will tell you when you can talk.

Example:

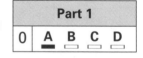

Part 1			
0	**A**	B	C	D

1

A Buy ten tickets and get one free.

B Tickets reserved today are cheaper.

C There are only ten tickets left.

D Some of our tickets are cheaper today.

2

This shop closes for lunch every day except Friday when we open all day

A This shop closes early on Fridays.

B We do not serve lunch on Fridays.

C This shop doesn't close for lunch on Fridays.

D We will not be open next Friday lunchtime.

3

Why not order your interval drinks before the concert?

A You cannot have a drink in the interval if you have not ordered it.

B You can get drinks both before and after the concert.

C You must finish your drink before you go into the concert.

D You can order drinks for the interval before you go in.

4

SWITCH OFF PRINTER BEFORE REMOVING BACK COVER

A Switch this printer off at the back.

B Do not take the back cover off the printer until it is turned off.

C Do not touch the switch at the back of this printer.

D Cover this printer up before you switch it on.

5

Mr. Hawksley's class is cancelled today as he is ill

A Do not come to the class if you are feeling ill.

B There is no class today because of Mr Hawksley's illness.

C Tell Mr Hawksley if you cannot come to the class.

D There will be an extra class for Mr Hawksley's students today.

PART 2

Questions 6–10

- The people below all want to go out somewhere.
- On the next page there are descriptions of eight places.
- Decide which place (**letters A–H**) would be the most suitable for each person (**numbers 6–10**).
- For each of these numbers mark the correct letter **on your answer sheet**.

Example:

Part 2							
0	A	B	C	D	E	F	G	H

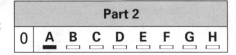

6  Alison has a friend coming to visit her on Saturday and would like to take her on an organised boat trip in the afternoon.

7  Martin has three children who love animals. He wants to take them out for the day and is looking for somewhere that has plenty for them to do where they can also have lunch.

8 Sarah is interested in the way people lived and worked in the past. She likes making things and would like to learn some of the old-fashioned skills people used to have.

9  David has just moved to the area and wants to find out more about it. He has Sunday mornings free but doesn't want to spend much.

10  Fiona's hobby is birdwatching. She is short of money but has a free weekend and wants to spend a quiet day in the open air enjoying the countryside and watching the birds.

A   The Leighton Lady is a luxury 54-seater pleasure boat and is available for hire – ideal for weddings, birthdays, etc. For the general public there are day trips on Sundays in summer and every day in August. Tel (01525) 384563 to book.

B   Whipsnade Animal Park is Europe's largest conservation park, offering:
- a fun and educational day out for all members of the family
- 3000 rare and endangered animals and birds

Open daily 10 a.m.–6 p.m. Phone (01582) 872171 for up-to-date admission charges.

C   Luton Museum includes a wide range of displays telling the story of Luton as an industrial centre up to the present day. Follow the history of some of Luton's industries and look inside a Victorian pub and shop. Open all year: Mon–Sat 10 a.m.–5 p.m., Sun 1–5 p.m. Admission free.

D   The Stockwood Craft Museum tells the history of traditional trades and crafts up until the 1930s. It offers a look back at arts such as weaving cloth and making pots. Watch the craftspeople at work and have a turn yourself! The Period Gardens show the history of English gardening from medieval times. Open Wed–Sun 10 a.m.–5 p.m.

E   Woodside Farm offers fun and enjoyment for all the family. Attractions include unusual breeds of farm animals, a children's farm, picnic/play areas, farm shop, tractor rides, pony rides, Coffee Pot café. Open all year: Mon–Sat 8 a.m.–5.30 p.m., closed Sunday. Admission Children and Senior Citizens £1.10, Adults £1.40.

F   Bedford Museum is in attractive surroundings close to the River Great Ouse. The excellent exhibitions show the human and natural history of the region. Find out, for example, what life was like in a village in Roman times or what wildlife and birds can be seen in the valley today. Open Tues–Sun 11 a.m.–5 p.m. Admission free.

G   Priory Country Park is a peaceful area just a short distance from Bedford town centre. The park, with lakes surrounded by trees and grassland, is a great place to see wildlife and birds. Priory Water Sports offers sailing and canoeing. Open all year. No entry charges.

H   Longholme Boating Lake offers safe boating for all the family in ten acres of beautiful parkland. Pedal boats, rowing boats and motorised children's boats are all available for hire. The lakeside cafe provides a range of refreshments. River trips leave on the hour from 1 p.m. at weekends.

PART 3

Questions 11–20

- Look at the statements below about a sports centre.
- Read the text on the next page to decide if each statement is correct or incorrect.
- If it is correct, mark **A on your answer sheet**.
- If it is not correct, mark **B on your answer sheet**.

Example:

11 You must become a member for at least one month.

12 Bookings must be made during the morning.

13 It is unnecessary for members to pay at the time of booking.

14 Only members can use courts booked in advance.

15 You'll have to pay extra if you don't show your membership card.

16 If you cancel the day before your booking, you must still pay.

17 You must attend at least two classes on the fitness machines to get your 'SKY' card.

18 Weight training is for people who want to get extra fit.

19 It costs more to do weight training alone than to attend the class.

20 All new members must attend classes before they can have a 'BLUE' card.

Aerobics, Archery, Badminton, Baseball, Fencing, Fitness Machines, Gymnastics, Handball, Judo, Karate, Netball, Roller Skating, Squash, Table Tennis, Tennis, Trampolining, Weight training

Sports Centre Membership Information

Membership includes the following benefits:
No entry fee.
Cheaper rates for use of equipment, courts, etc.
Book up to ten days in advance.

Cost of Membership

Family	6 months: £34	
	12 months: £58	
Adult	Day membership: 65p	
	1 month: £3	
	6 months: £18	
	1 year: £36	
Junior	Day membership: 40p	
	6 months: £8	
	1 year: £13	

Rules of Membership

- Members may book courts, etc. by telephone 9.30 a.m.–10.30 p.m. seven days a week up to ten days in advance. Membership number must be given when booking by phone and payment made immediately on arrival at the sports centre. A booking made in this way may only be used by the member and his/her guest or guests.
- Members need not pay day membership fees provided that they can produce a membership card. Failure to do so will result in a day membership fee and full cost for use of any equipment, courts, etc. being charged.
- Bookings may be cancelled up to 48 hours before the day, otherwise the hire fee will be charged plus an administrative charge.

Fitness Machines

These machines will help you to work almost every muscle in your body. Before training by yourself, it is necessary to come to a minimum course of two classes which will give you the 'SKY' card so that you can train whenever you like. One-hour classes are held every week on Monday and Friday at 12 noon and 9 p.m. Fee per class: Member £2.15, Non-member £5.00. Individual training fees (after receipt of 'SKY' or 'BLUE' card only): Member £2.10 per hour, Non-member £3.20 per hour.

Weight Training

If you would like to become a little more serious about the shape of your body, then our weight training room is for you. This area allows you to train using 'free' weights as well as machines and can help you to reach a really high level of physical fitness. Before training here, you must first attend classes to obtain your 'SKY' card (see Fitness Machines), followed by a minimum of two further classes to gain your 'BLUE' card which will allow you to train on your own. For fees, see Fitness Machines above.

However, if you are an experienced weight trainer, then it may not be necessary for you to come to classes. Consultation with one of our instructors will provide more advice on this matter. If it is not necessary for you to take any classes, your first weight training session will cost £6, which includes your 'BLUE' card.

PART 4

Questions 21–25

- Read the text and questions below.
- For each question, mark the letter next to the correct answer – **A**, **B**, **C** or **D** –
  on your answer sheet.

Example:

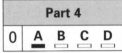

> I know that it is my job to make sure that everything goes
> well for the tourists and I feel I work hard for the
> company. I cannot be blamed for last week. I met the group
> at the airport and took them to the coach. The coach
> driver was a bit annoyed because the flight was late. But
> it wasn't far to the hotel and everyone was looking
> forward to their dinner. We hadn't used the Hotel Riviera
> before but our normal one had a conference in it so was
> fully booked. When I announced our arrival at the
> reception desk, they said they were full. I had booked
> rooms for the group but the manager said they were
> cancelled by phone a few days before. He insisted that he
> recognised my voice and that I had made the phone call. We
> had a bit of an argument but they obviously didn't have
> enough rooms. In the end the manager phoned other hotels
> in the town and found rooms for everyone but in four
> different hotels. By this time the coach had gone so we
> had to get taxis and some of the tourists started to get
> very angry with me. I still don't know who made that phone
> call but it definitely wasn't me.

21 What is the writer trying to do?

    A   argue

    B   apologise

    C   explain

    D   complain

22 Who was the text written to?

    A   one of the tourists

    B   the writer's employer

    C   the hotel manager

    D   the coach company

23 Why weren't any rooms available at the Hotel Riviera?

A A conference was taking place there.
B There were more people in the group than expected.
C Someone had forgotten to book them.
D Someone had said they were not needed.

24 What happened in the end?

A The tourists got angry with the hotel manager.
B The tourists couldn't stay together.
C The writer found other hotels with rooms.
D The writer called the coach driver back.

25 Which of the following diaries was written by one of the tourists?

A
> Someone had made a mistake with our hotel booking and the hotel had given our rooms to other people.

B
> The hotel we were taken to wasn't good enough so we asked to change to a different one.

C
> We got to the airport and had to wait for the coach. So it was really late when we got to the hotel.

D
> The coach driver took us to the wrong hotel and they knew nothing about us.

PART 5

Questions 26–35

- Read the text below and choose the correct word for each space.
- For each question, mark the letter next to the correct word – **A**, **B**, **C** or **D** – **on your answer sheet**.

Example:

Part 5				
0	A	B	C	D

STARTING A BUSINESS

Nearly 450,000 businesses are started in Britain **(0)** .... year. One third **(26)** .... these stops trading during the first three years.

    Starting a business is never easy **(27)** .... so many things are outside your control. If you are thinking about working for yourself, you **(28)** .... start by thinking about the qualities you need to **(29)** .... a business. Be hard with yourself. If you have a weakness, it is better to find out now **(30)** .... than later when your business could be in danger. Ask yourself **(31)** .... you are a good organiser. Is your health **(32)** .... ? Are you good **(33)** .... making decisions? Do you have any practical experience of the business you want to start? Are you prepared to work long hours for very **(34)** .... money? If you can't **(35)** .... yes to most of these questions, perhaps you should think again about starting up in business on your own.

---

(0)	**A** every	**B** this	**C** last	**D** one
26	**A** from	**B** of	**C** among	**D** in
27	**A** however	**B** but	**C** because	**D** although
28	**A** have	**B** ought	**C** need	**D** must
29	**A** run	**B** make	**C** do	**D** set
30	**A** more	**B** rather	**C** earlier	**D** quicker
31	**A** which	**B** how	**C** whether	**D** that
32	**A** fine	**B** firm	**C** well	**D** good
33	**A** at	**B** for	**C** in	**D** with
34	**A** short	**B** little	**C** low	**D** few
35	**A** give	**B** report	**C** answer	**D** put

WRITING

PART 1

Questions 1–5

- Here are some sentences about a library.
- For each question, finish the second sentence so that it means the same as the first.
- The second sentence is started for you. **Write only the missing words on your answer sheet**.
- You may use this page for any rough work.

> **Example:**   The library was opened by the college president.
>
> **The college president** *opened the library.*

1   The librarian told Danny to return the book on Monday.

The librarian said: 'You ....

2   There are 80,000 books in this library.

The library ....

3   The library lends books to both students and teachers.

Both students and teachers can ....

4   The science librarian is more helpful than the history librarian.

The history librarian ....

5   If you lose your library card, there is a charge of £2.

If you lose your library card, you must ....

PART 2

Questions 6–15

- An international video company wants to find out about TV audiences.
- You have agreed to help them.
- Look at the questionnaire and answer each question.
- **Write your answers on your answer sheet**.
- You may use this page for any rough work.

CBTV world entertainments network

name: **(6)** ....

address: **(7)** ....

....

age: **(8)** ....   sex: **(9)** ....

how many hours per week do you spend watching

television? **(10)** ....

which day(s) do you watch most television?

(11) ....

please give your <u>2 favourite</u> types of television programme:

(12) ....   **(13)** ....

which type of programme do you like <u>least</u>?

(14) ....

SIGNATURE **(15)** ....

PART 3

Question 16

- You've just been on a visit to another country.
- You are writing a letter to your English penfriend.
- You want to describe what you saw and how you felt.
- You can use some ideas from the pictures if you wish.
- **Finish the letter on your answer sheet, using about 100 words.**
- You may use this page for any rough work.

Dear .... ,
I'm writing to tell you about my trip abroad last month.

....

....

....

....

....

....

....

....

....

....

PAPER 2   Listening Test   Approx 30 minutes
(+12 minutes transfer time)

PART 1

Questions 1–7

- There are seven questions in this Part.
- For each question there are four pictures and a short recording.
- You will hear each recording twice.
- For each question, look at the pictures and listen to the recording.
- Choose the correct picture and put a tick (✓) in the box below it.

Example: What should the class do?

 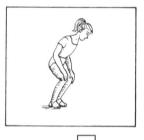  

A ✓   B ☐   C ☐   D ☐

1   What is wrong with her?

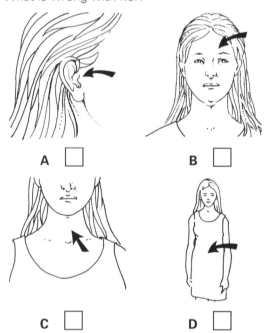

A ☐   B ☐

C ☐   D ☐

2   What's Alice going to do this afternoon?

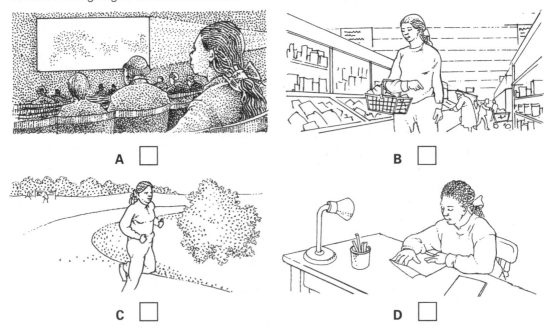

A ☐   B ☐

C ☐   D ☐

3   What was the weather like?

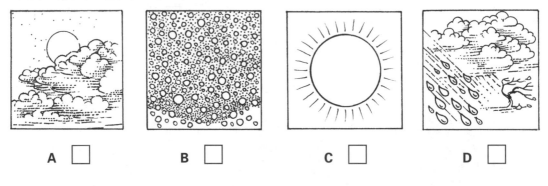

A ☐   B ☐   C ☐   D ☐

4   Where is he putting the television?

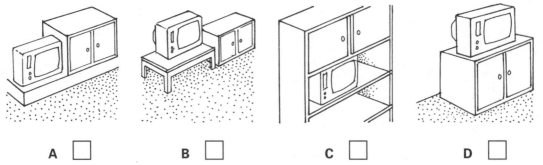

A ☐   B ☐   C ☐   D ☐

5 Which sport does she do now?

A ☐   B ☐   C ☐   D ☐

6 Which is the manager?

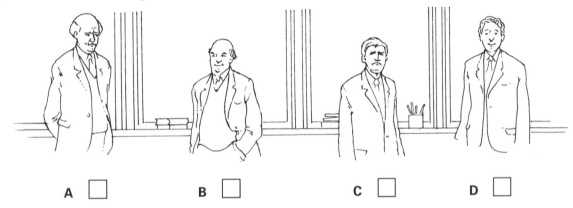

A ☐   B ☐   C ☐   D ☐

7 Which is the house?

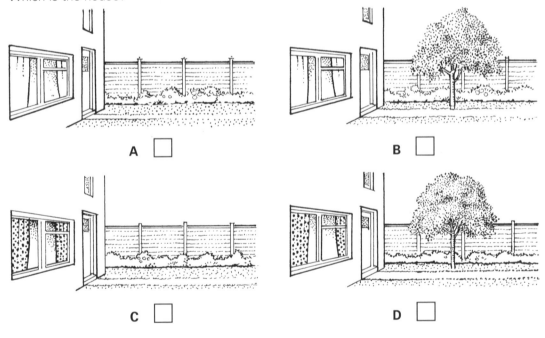

A ☐

B ☐

C ☐

D ☐

PART 2

Questions 8–13

- Look at the questions for this Part.
- You will hear someone talking about jobs for young people in Australia.
- Put a tick (✔) in the correct box for each question.

8 BUNAC will help you if you

A ☐ come from any European country.

B ☐ are at least 21.

C ☐ have a certain amount of money.

D ☐ have some work experience.

9 BUNAC cannot help with

A ☐ finding you accommodation on arrival.

B ☐ finding you accommodation for your stay.

C ☐ arranging flights.

D ☐ arranging insurance.

10 The Australian Trust for the Environment can find you a job if you

A ☐ are in good health.

B ☐ have worked on a farm before.

C ☐ can speak several languages.

D ☐ agree to stay for six months.

11 There are jobs available picking tobacco in January in

A ☐ central Victoria.

B ☐ northern Victoria.

C ☐ central Queensland.

D ☐ northern Queensland.

12 In February and March you can help to pick

A ☐ pineapples.

B ☐ bananas.

C ☐ grapes.

D ☐ tobacco.

13 If you want more information, you should

A ☐ phone for a booklet.

B ☐ write for a booklet.

C ☐ take a booklet.

D ☐ fill in a form.

PART 3

Questions 14–19

- Look at the notes.
- Some information is missing.
- You will hear a student talking to her class about a famous person.
- For each question, fill in the missing information in the numbered space.

<u>Florence Nightingale</u>

Born 1820 in (14) ....

Parents were (15) .... English people.

1845 went to train as a nurse in (16) ....

1853 became head of a (17) .... hospital in London.

Became famous for looking after (18) .... abroad.

Believed nurses should always think about the (19) .... of patients.

PART 4

Questions 20–25

- Look at the six statements for this Part.
- You will hear a conversation between a boy, John, and a girl, Katie.
- Decide if you think each statement is correct or incorrect.
- If you think it is correct, put a tick (✓) in the box under **A** for **YES**. If you think it is not correct, put a tick (✓) in the box under **B** for **NO**.

		A YES	B NO
20	Anna is Italian.	☐	☐
21	Anna tried to speak English with her friends.	☐	☐
22	Anna often speaks Italian in front of Katie.	☐	☐
23	Anna's Italian friends arrived suddenly.	☐	☐
24	John understands Anna's point of view.	☐	☐
25	Katie would like to be friends with the Italians.	☐	☐

About the Speaking test

The Speaking test lasts about 10 or 12 minutes. You usually do the Speaking test at the same time as another candidate. There are two examiners but probably only one of them will talk to you. The examiner sometimes asks you a question and sometimes asks you to talk to the other candidate.

Part 1

The examiner says hello and asks each of you to say your name, candidate number and nationality. The examiner then asks you to talk to the other candidate and find out more information about him or her. You must also answer the questions the other candidate asks you.

Part 2

The examiner gives you and the other candidate some pictures, drawings or advertisements to look at. Together you talk about what you can see.

Part 3

The examiner gives each of you a colour photograph to look at. You take turns to talk about your own photograph.

Part 4

The examiner asks you and the other candidate to say more about the subject of the photograph in Part 3. You may be asked for your opinion or to talk about something that has happened to you.

Note: If you do the Speaking test alone, it is similar but you talk to the examiner instead of another candidate.

Sample answer sheets

CAMBRIDGE
EXAMINATIONS, CERTIFICATES AND DIPLOMAS
ENGLISH AS A FOREIGN LANGUAGE

University of Cambridge
Local Examinations Syndicate
International Examinations

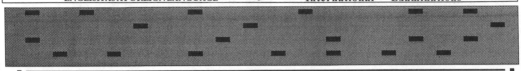

For Supervisor's use only
Shade here if the candidate is **ABSENT** or has **WITHDRAWN**
➡ ▭ ↩

Examination Details   9999/01   99/D99

Examination Title   Preliminary English Test

Centre/Candidate No.   AA999/9999

Candidate Name   A.N. EXAMPLE

• Sign here if the details above are correct

☒

- -
• Tell the Supervisor now if the details above are not correct

PET READING ANSWER SHEET

Use a pencil

Mark one letter for each question.

For example:

If you think A is the right answer to the question, mark your answer sheet like this:

| 0 | A ▬ |

Change your answer like this:

Part 1	Part 2	Part 3	Part 4	Part 5
1 A B C D	6 A B C D E F G H	11 A B	21 A B C D	26 A B C D
2 A B C D	7 A B C D E F G H	12 A B	22 A B C D	27 A B C D
3 A B C D	8 A B C D E F G H	13 A B	23 A B C D	28 A B C D
4 A B C D	9 A B C D E F G H	14 A B	24 A B C D	29 A B C D
5 A B C D	10 A B C D E F G H	15 A B	25 A B C D	30 A B C D
		16 A B		31 A B C D
		17 A B		32 A B C D
		18 A B		33 A B C D
		19 A B		34 A B C D
		20 A B		35 A B C D

You may photocopy this page.

© UCLES/K&J

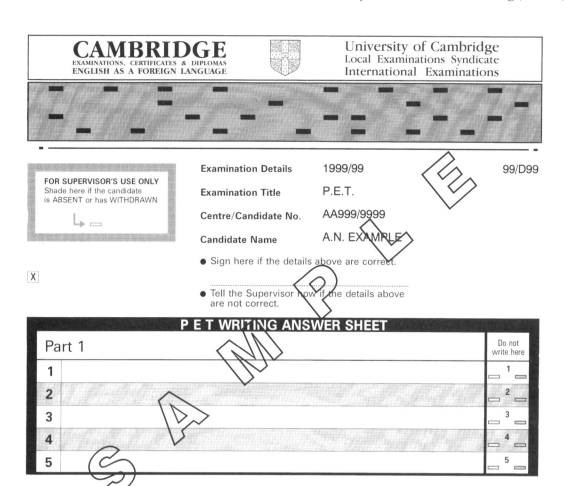

© UCLES/K&J

Part 3: Write your answer in the box below

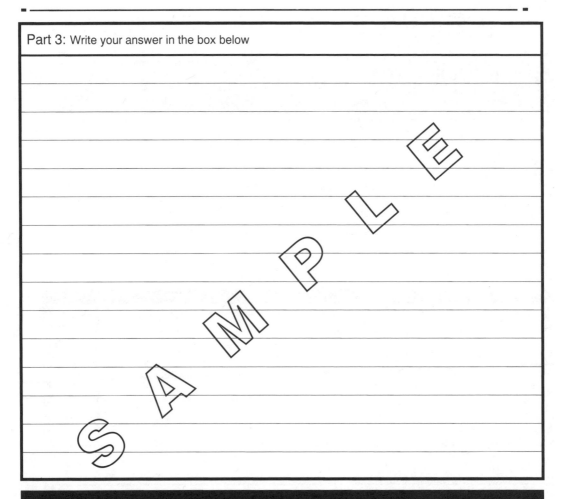

Do not write below this line

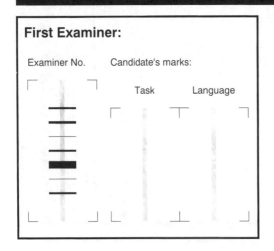

First Examiner:

Examiner No.   Candidate's marks:

                        Task   Language

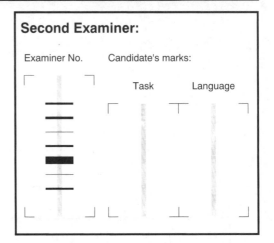

Second Examiner:

Examiner No.   Candidate's marks:

                        Task   Language

© UCLES/K&J

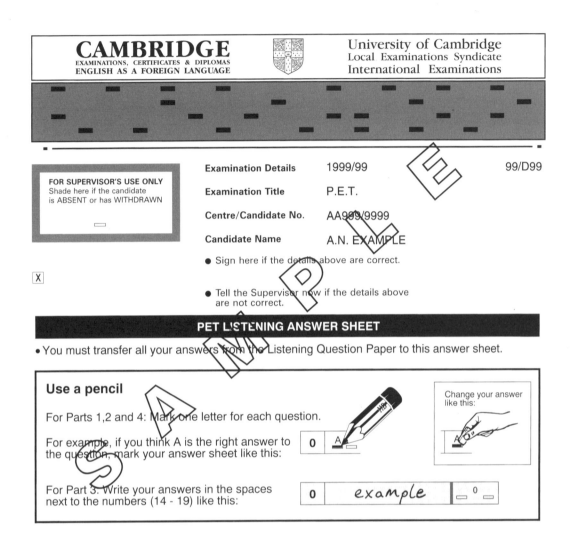

CAMBRIDGE
EXAMINATIONS, CERTIFICATES & DIPLOMAS
ENGLISH AS A FOREIGN LANGUAGE

University of Cambridge
Local Examinations Syndicate
International Examinations

FOR SUPERVISOR'S USE ONLY
Shade here if the candidate
is ABSENT or has WITHDRAWN

Examination Details	1999/99	99/D99
Examination Title	P.E.T.	
Centre/Candidate No.	AA999/9999	
Candidate Name	A.N. EXAMPLE	

X

● Sign here if the details above are correct.

● Tell the Supervisor now if the details above
  are not correct.

PET LISTENING ANSWER SHEET

• You must transfer all your answers from the Listening Question Paper to this answer sheet.

Use a pencil

For Parts 1,2 and 4: Mark one letter for each question.

For example, if you think A is the right answer to the question, mark your answer sheet like this:

0 | A

Change your answer
like this:

For Part 3: Write your answers in the spaces next to the numbers (14 - 19) like this:

0 | *example* | 0

	Part 1		Part 2		Part 3	Do not write here		Part 4
1	A B C D	8	A B C D	14		14	20	A B
2	A B C D	9	A B C D	15		15	21	A B
3	A B C D	10	A B C D	16		16	22	A B
4	A B C D	11	A B C D	17		17	23	A B
5	A B C D	12	A B C D	18		18	24	A B
6	A B C D	13	A B C D	19		19	25	A B
7	A B C D							

You may photocopy this page.

© UCLES/K&J

121

Acknowledgements

The authors and publishers are grateful to the following individuals and institutions for permission to reproduce copyright photographs. It has not been possible to identify the sources of all the material used and in such cases the publishers would welcome information from copyright holders.

Abbas Hashemi on pp. 1, 3, 4, 38, 39, 58, 59, 78, 79, 98, 99; The Image Bank/Bokelberg on p. 69; Jeremy Pembrey on pp. 37, 49.

Colour section: photographs by Ace Photo Agency/Ian Reynolds (1B left); Art Directors Photo Library (2B); Tom Webster/Impact Photos (4D); Jeremy Pembrey (1C, 1D, 5C, 5D); Spectrum Colour Library (1A left); Telegraph Colour Library/ R. Jewell (2C), Trip/J. Highet (1A right); Viewfinder Colour Photo Library (4C, 1B right); Elizabeth Whiting & Associates (3C, 3D).

Picture research by Sandie Huskinson-Rolf (PHOTOSEEKERS).

The sample answer sheets on pages 118–121 are reproduced by kind permission of the University of Cambridge Local Examinations Syndicate.

Drawings by David Byatt (e.g. p. 24), David Cook (e.g. p. 52), David Downton (e.g. p. 6) and Linda Worrell (e.g. p. 27).

Book design by Peter Ducker MSTD.